Presented To
Cedar Mill Community Library

Donated

by

Paul Sawyer

& Applied Materials

Pebble® Plus

AFRICAN ANIMALS
Leopards

by Deborah Nuzzolo

Consulting Editor: Gail Saunders-Smith, PhD

Consultant:
George Wittemyer, PhD
NSF International Postdoctoral Fellow
University of California at Berkeley

Capstone press®

Mankato, Minnesota

Pebble Plus is published by Capstone Press,
151 Good Counsel Drive, P.O. Box 669, Mankato, Minnesota 56002.
www.capstonepub.com

 Books published by Capstone Press are manufactured with paper
containing at least 10 percent post-consumer waste.

Library of Congress Cataloging-in-Publication Data
Nuzzolo, Deborah.
    Leopards / by Deborah Nuzzolo.
    p. cm. — (Pebble plus. African animals)
    Includes bibliographical references and index.
    ISBN-13: 978-1-4296-1247-0 (library binding)
    ISBN-13: 978-1-4296-4881-3 (paperback)
    1. Leopard — Africa — Juvenile literature. I. Title. II. Series.
QL737.C23N89 2008
599.75'54096 — dc22   2007028677

Summary: Discusses leopards, their African habitat, food, and behavior.

Editorial Credits
Erika L. Shores, editor; Renée T. Doyle, set designer; Laura Manthe, photo researcher

Photo Credits
Afripics.com, 18–19
Art Life Images/Fritz Polking, 5; Werner Bollmann, 16–17
BigStockPhoto.com/Johan Swanepoel, 20–21
Creatas, 1
Dreamstime/Pshaw-photo, 13
fotolia/Stefanie Van der Vinden, 6–7
iStockphoto/Kristian Sekulic, cover; Nico Smit, 8–9
Jupiter Images, 10–11
Shutterstock/Kristian Sekulic, 22; photobar, cover, 1, 3 (fur)
Visuals Unlimited/Fritz Polking, 14–15

Note to Parents and Teachers

The African Animals set supports national science standards related to life science.
This book describes and illustrates leopards. The images support early readers in
understanding the text. The repetition of words and phrases helps early readers learn
new words. This book also introduces early readers to subject-specific vocabulary words,
which are defined in the Glossary section. Early readers may need assistance to read some
words and to use the Table of Contents, Glossary, Read More, Internet Sites, and Index
sections of the book.

Printed in the United States of America in North Mankato, Minnesota.
102010
005971R

Table of Contents

Living in Africa

Leopards step silently through Africa's grasslands and forests.

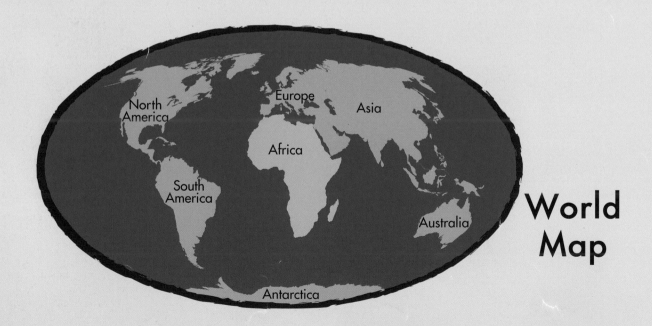

World Map

Leopards stay cool
in Africa's heat.
They rest in the shade.

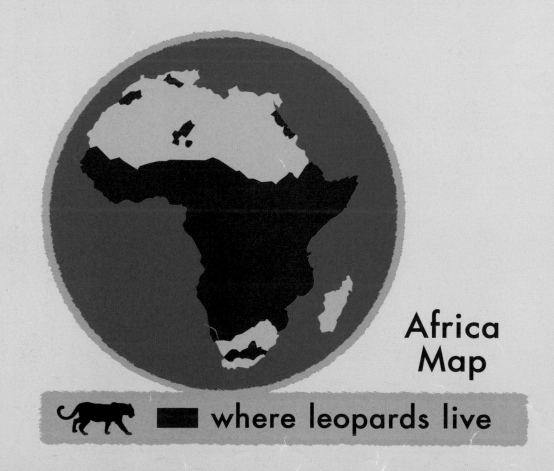

Africa
Map

 ■ where leopards live

Up Close!

Can you find the leopard?
Its spotted coat blends in
with rocks and tall grass.

Leopards have strong legs.

They use their legs

to climb tall trees.

Eating and Drinking

Shh! It's night.

Leopards are awake.

They hunt for antelope,

birds, and small mammals.

Lions and hyenas try to steal

a leopard's meal.

The leopard hides its food

high up in trees.

Splash!

Leopards like water.

They jump in to find fish

or to take a drink.

Staying Safe

A mother leopard keeps
her cubs safe from predators.
She hides them in trees
and dens.

It's daytime.

Leopards sleep safe

and snug in Africa's trees.

Glossary

antelope — an animal that looks like a large deer and runs very fast

den — a place where a wild animal lives

grassland — a flat area of grassy land

mammal — a warm-blooded animal with fur; female mammals feed milk to their young.

predator — an animal that hunts other animals for food

shade — an area that is out of the sun

Read More

Cooper, Jason. *Leopards*. Eye to Eye with Big Cats. Vero Beach, Fla.: Rourke, 2003.

Squire, Ann O. *Leopards*. A True Book. New York: Children's Press, 2005.

Zumbusch, Amelia von. *Leopards: Silent Stalkers*. Dangerous Cats. New York: PowerKid's Press, 2007.

Internet Sites

FactHound offers a safe, fun way to find Internet sites related to this book. All of the sites on FactHound have been researched by our staff.

Here's how:

1. Visit *www.facthound.com*

2. Choose your grade level.

3. Type in this book ID **1429612479** for age-appropriate sites. You may also browse subjects by clicking on letters, or by clicking on pictures and words.

4. Click on the **Fetch It** button.

FactHound will fetch the best sites for you!

Index

Word Count: 119
Grade: 1
Early-Intervention Level: 16

LEISURE ARTS PRESENTS

christmas keepsakes

*'Tis the season
... to remember.*

LEISURE ARTS, INC.
Little Rock, Arkansas

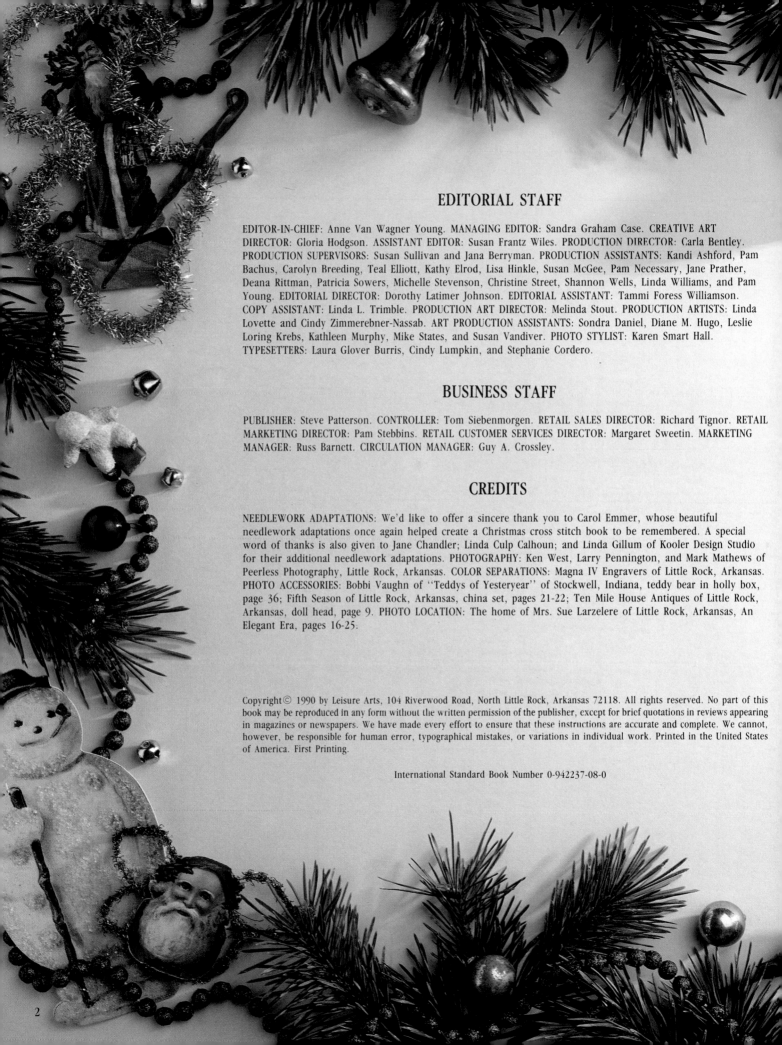

EDITORIAL STAFF

EDITOR-IN-CHIEF: Anne Van Wagner Young. MANAGING EDITOR: Sandra Graham Case. CREATIVE ART DIRECTOR: Gloria Hodgson. ASSISTANT EDITOR: Susan Frantz Wiles. PRODUCTION DIRECTOR: Carla Bentley. PRODUCTION SUPERVISORS: Susan Sullivan and Jana Berryman. PRODUCTION ASSISTANTS: Kandi Ashford, Pam Bachus, Carolyn Breeding, Teal Elliott, Kathy Elrod, Lisa Hinkle, Susan McGee, Pam Necessary, Jane Prather, Deana Rittman, Patricia Sowers, Michelle Stevenson, Christine Street, Shannon Wells, Linda Williams, and Pam Young. EDITORIAL DIRECTOR: Dorothy Latimer Johnson. EDITORIAL ASSISTANT: Tammi Foress Williamson. COPY ASSISTANT: Linda L. Trimble. PRODUCTION ART DIRECTOR: Melinda Stout. PRODUCTION ARTISTS: Linda Lovette and Cindy Zimmerebner-Nassab. ART PRODUCTION ASSISTANTS: Sondra Daniel, Diane M. Hugo, Leslie Loring Krebs, Kathleen Murphy, Mike States, and Susan Vandiver. PHOTO STYLIST: Karen Smart Hall. TYPESETTERS: Laura Glover Burris, Cindy Lumpkin, and Stephanie Cordero.

BUSINESS STAFF

PUBLISHER: Steve Patterson. CONTROLLER: Tom Siebenmorgen. RETAIL SALES DIRECTOR: Richard Tignor. RETAIL MARKETING DIRECTOR: Pam Stebbins. RETAIL CUSTOMER SERVICES DIRECTOR: Margaret Sweetin. MARKETING MANAGER: Russ Barnett. CIRCULATION MANAGER: Guy A. Crossley.

CREDITS

NEEDLEWORK ADAPTATIONS: We'd like to offer a sincere thank you to Carol Emmer, whose beautiful needlework adaptations once again helped create a Christmas cross stitch book to be remembered. A special word of thanks is also given to Jane Chandler; Linda Culp Calhoun; and Linda Gillum of Kooler Design Studio for their additional needlework adaptations. PHOTOGRAPHY: Ken West, Larry Pennington, and Mark Mathews of Peerless Photography, Little Rock, Arkansas. COLOR SEPARATIONS: Magna IV Engravers of Little Rock, Arkansas. PHOTO ACCESSORIES: Bobbi Vaughn of "Teddys of Yesteryear" of Stockwell, Indiana, teddy bear in holly box, page 36; Fifth Season of Little Rock, Arkansas, china set, pages 21-22; Ten Mile House Antiques of Little Rock, Arkansas, doll head, page 9. PHOTO LOCATION: The home of Mrs. Sue Larzelere of Little Rock, Arkansas, An Elegant Era, pages 16-25.

International Standard Book Number 0-942237-08-0

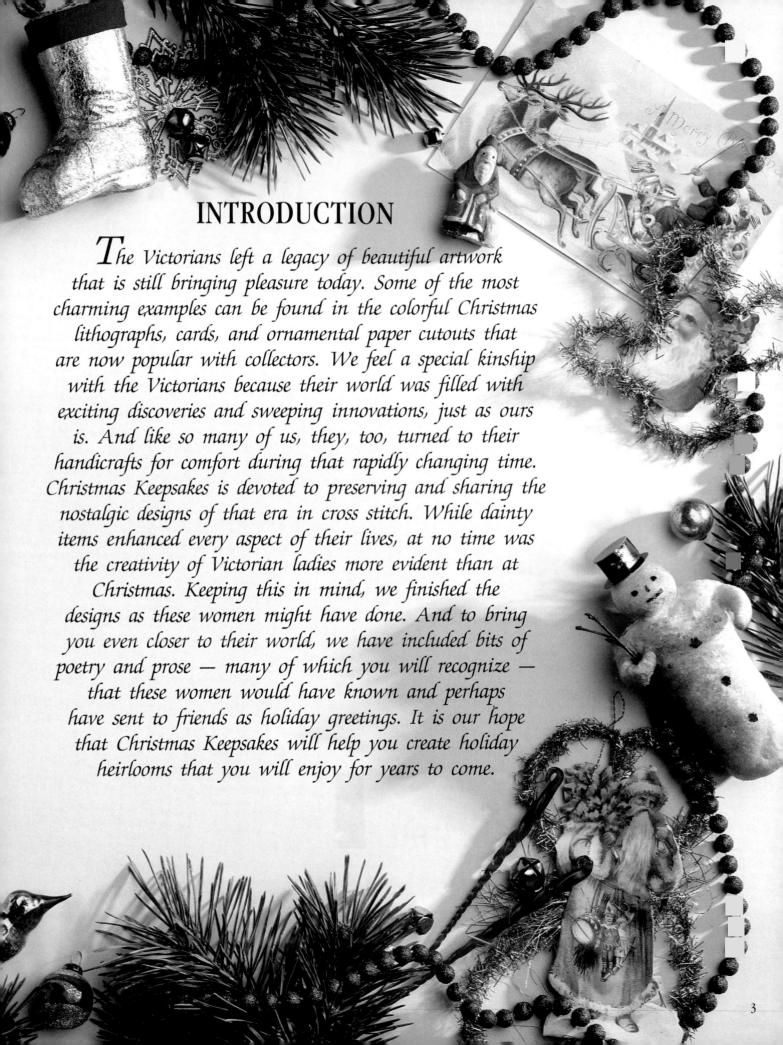

INTRODUCTION

The Victorians left a legacy of beautiful artwork that is still bringing pleasure today. Some of the most charming examples can be found in the colorful Christmas lithographs, cards, and ornamental paper cutouts that are now popular with collectors. We feel a special kinship with the Victorians because their world was filled with exciting discoveries and sweeping innovations, just as ours is. And like so many of us, they, too, turned to their handicrafts for comfort during that rapidly changing time. Christmas Keepsakes is devoted to preserving and sharing the nostalgic designs of that era in cross stitch. While dainty items enhanced every aspect of their lives, at no time was the creativity of Victorian ladies more evident than at Christmas. Keeping this in mind, we finished the designs as these women might have done. And to bring you even closer to their world, we have included bits of poetry and prose — many of which you will recognize — that these women would have known and perhaps have sent to friends as holiday greetings. It is our hope that Christmas Keepsakes will help you create holiday heirlooms that you will enjoy for years to come.

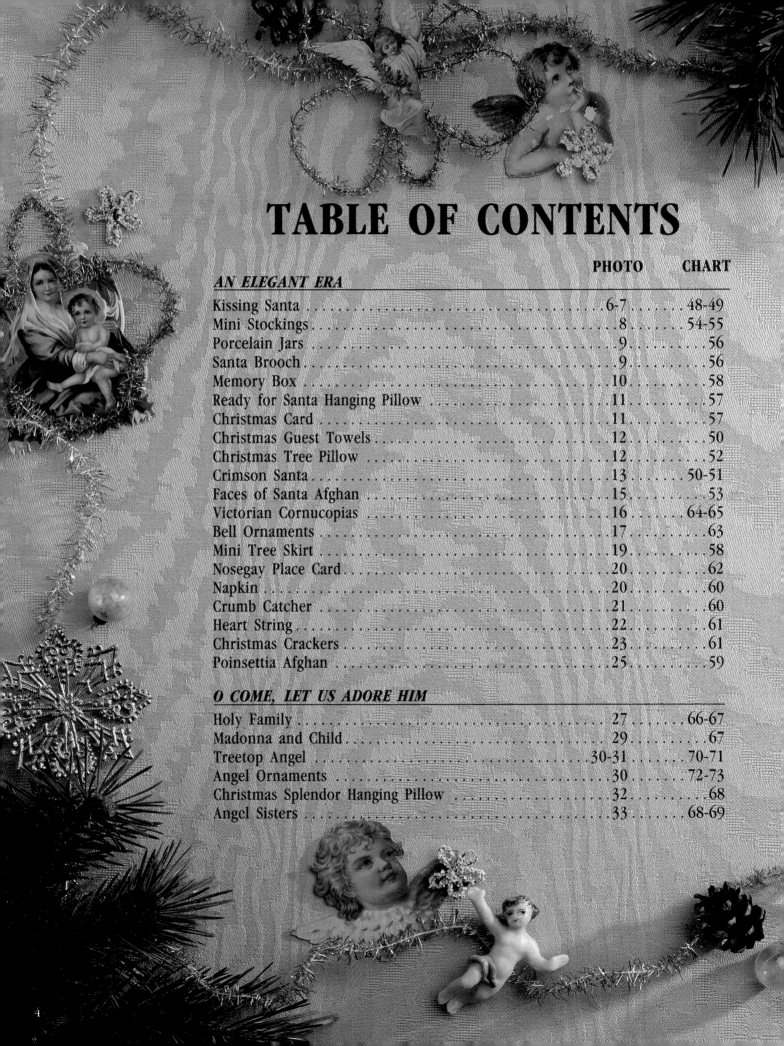

TABLE OF CONTENTS

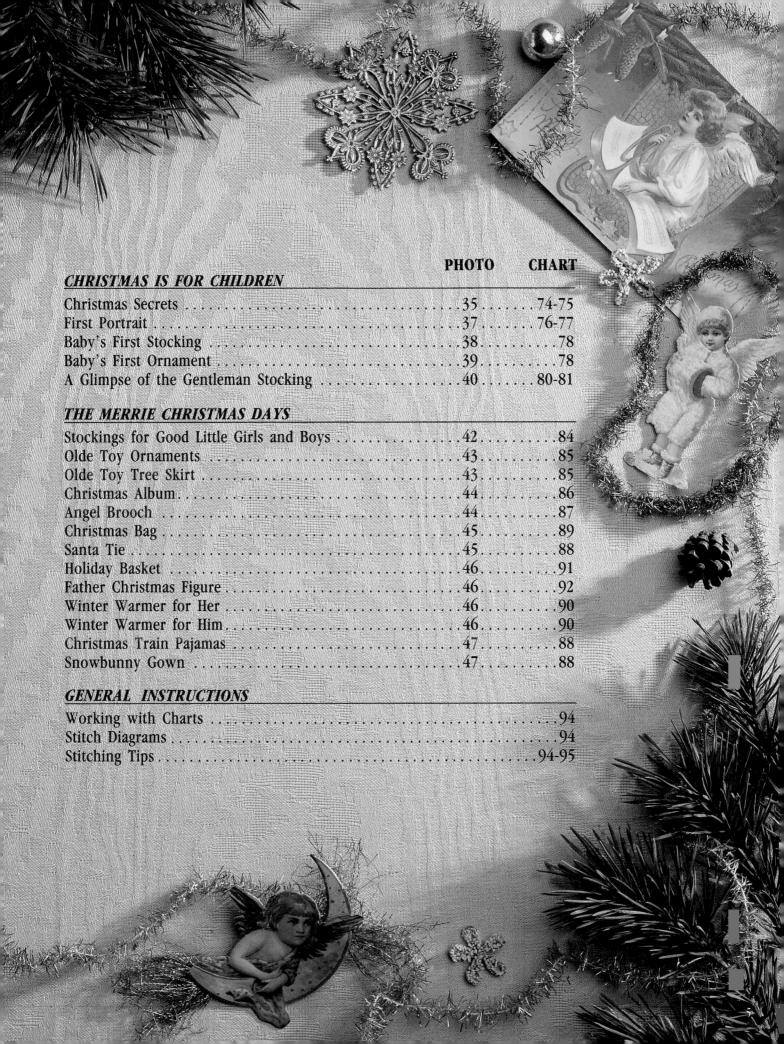

an Elegant Era

*The children's day
again is here,
The gladdest day
of all the year,
Of old delights,
and pleasures new,
May it hold goodly
store for you.*

Chart: Kissing Santa, pages 48-49

The stockings hang o'er
fire-place glowing,
That tenderest hands with
gifts shall fill,
Each token, from the
heart, bestowing
The love that the
Christmas hours instill.

May your Christmas Day be blest With those things you like the best.

Charts: Mini Stockings, pages 54-55; Porcelain Jars and Santa Brooch, page 56

9

This brings my dearest love to you,
And greetings warm and hearty —
The merriest of Christmas Days —
To you and all your party.

Charts: Memory Box, page 58;
Ready for Santa Hanging Pillow
and Christmas Card, page 57

11

Now gay trees rise
Before your eyes,
Abloom with
tempting cheer;
Blithe voices sing
And blithe bells ring
For Christmastide
Is here.

— OLD ENGLISH CAROL

Charts: Christmas Guest Towels, page 50;
Christmas Tree Pillow, page 52;
Crimson Santa, pages 50-51

Santa, the children's good old friend,
With expectations without end,
May cheer your home this Christmas-Day,
Bring you Good Luck to stay for aye.

Chart: Faces of Santa Afghan, page 53

15

I heard the bells on Christmas Day
Their old, familiar carols play,
And wild and sweet the words repeat
Of peace on earth, good-will to men.

Then pealed the bells more loud and deep:
"God is not dead, nor doth He sleep:
The wrong shall fail, the right prevail,
With peace on earth, good-will to men."

— *HENRY WADSWORTH LONGFELLOW*

Charts: Victorian Cornucopias, pages 64-65;
Bell Ornaments, page 63

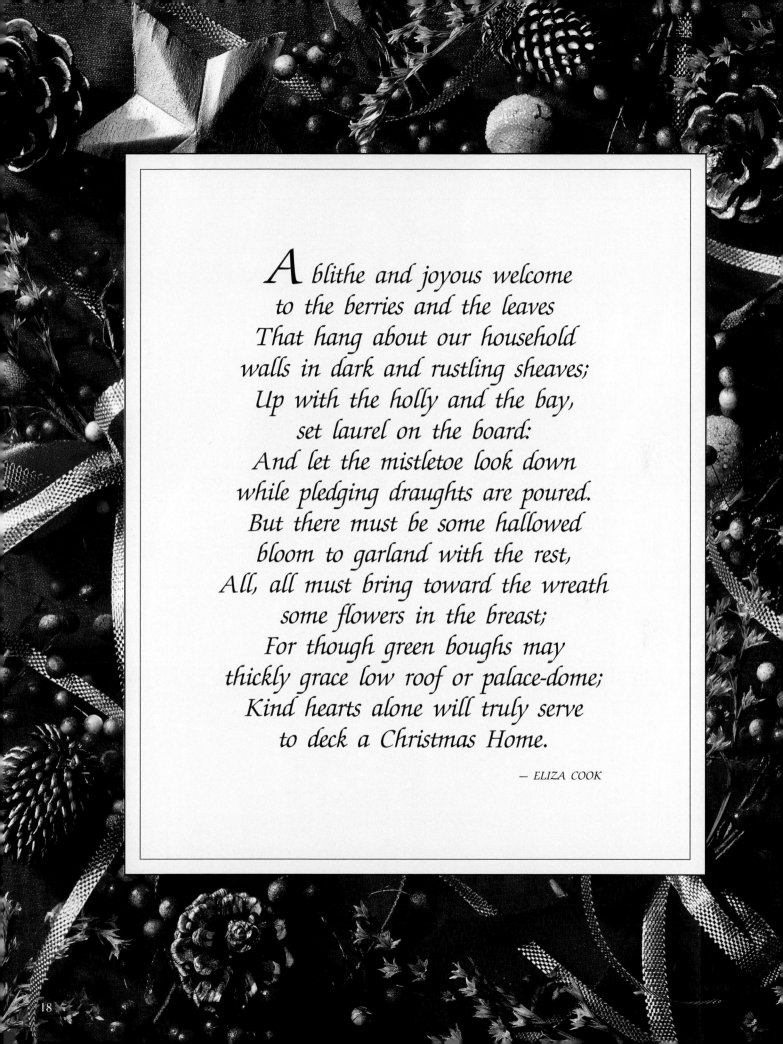

A blithe and joyous welcome
to the berries and the leaves
That hang about our household
walls in dark and rustling sheaves;
Up with the holly and the bay,
set laurel on the board:
And let the mistletoe look down
while pledging draughts are poured.
But there must be some hallowed
bloom to garland with the rest,
All, all must bring toward the wreath
some flowers in the breast;
For though green boughs may
thickly grace low roof or palace-dome;
Kind hearts alone will truly serve
to deck a Christmas Home.

— *ELIZA COOK*

Chart: Mini Tree Skirt, page 58

19

*A day of joy and feasting
Of happiness and mirth;
And every year it cometh here
To gladden all the earth.*

Charts: Nosegay Place Card, page 62;
Napkin and Crumb Catcher, page 60

It is a beautiful arrangement, also, derived from days of yore, that this festival, which commemorates the announcement of the religion of peace and love, has been made the season for gathering together of family connections, and drawing closer again those bands of kindred hearts.

— WASHINGTON IRVING

Charts: Heart String and Christmas Crackers, page 61

23

We bring in the holly,
the ivy, the pine,
The spruce and the hemlock
together we twine;
With evergreen branches
our walls we array
For the keeping of Christmas,
our high holiday.
Glory to God in the highest
we sing,
Peace and good-will are the
tidings we bring.

— OLD ENGLISH CAROL

24

Chart: Poinsettia Afghan, page 59

25

O Come, Let Us Adore Him

For unto us a child is born,
unto us a son is given:
and the government shall be
upon his shoulder: and his name
shall be called Wonderful,
Counsellor, The mighty God,
The everlasting Father,
The Prince of Peace.

— ISAIAH 9:6

Chart: Holy Family, pages 66-67

27

And it came to pass in those days, that there went out a decree from Caesar Augustus, that all the world should be taxed. And all went to be taxed, every one into his own city. And Joseph also went up from Galilee, out of the city of Nazareth, into Judaea, unto the city of David, which is called Bethlehem; (because he was of the house and lineage of David:) To be taxed with Mary his espoused wife, being great with child. And so it was, that, while they were there, the days were accomplished that she should be delivered. And she brought forth her firstborn son, and wrapped him in swaddling clothes, and laid him in a manger; because there was no room for them in the inn. And there were in the same country shepherds abiding in the field, keeping watch over their flock by night. And, lo, the angel of the Lord came upon them, and the glory of the Lord shone round about them: and they were sore afraid. And the angel said unto them, Fear not: for, behold, I bring you good tidings of great joy, which shall be to all people. For unto you is born this day in the city of David a Saviour, which is Christ the Lord.

— LUKE 2:1–11

GOD BLESS THEE

To wish you a happy Christmas

28

Chart: Madonna and Child, page 67

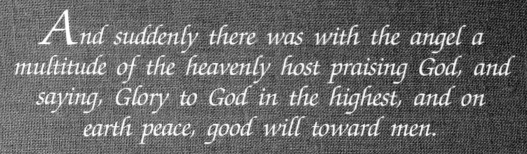

*A*nd suddenly there was with the angel a multitude of the heavenly host praising God, and saying, Glory to God in the highest, and on earth peace, good will toward men.

— LUKE 2:13-14

Charts: Treetop Angel, pages 70-71;
Angel Ornaments, pages 72-73

It is good to be children sometimes, and never better than at Christmas when its mighty Founder was a child Himself.

— *CHARLES DICKENS*

Hello Little One:

*I am coming to see you
Christmas Eve, so go to bed early,
after hanging up your stocking.*

*Yours truly,
Santa Claus*

Chart: First Portrait, pages 76-77

In every baby-face that comes,
God still is near.

— J. PAGE HOPPS

Chart: Baby's First Stocking and
Baby's First Ornament, page 78

Chart: A Glimpse of the Gentleman Stocking, pages 80-81

40

ϒes, Virginia, there is a Santa Claus. He exists as certainly as love and generosity and devotion exist, and you know that they abound and give to your life its highest beauty and joy. Alas! how dreary would be the world if there were no Santa Claus! It would be as dreary as if there were no Virginias. There would be no childlike faith then, no poetry, no romance to make tolerable this existence. We should have no enjoyment, except in sense and sight. The eternal light with which childhood fills the world would be extinguished. Not believe in Santa Claus! You might as well not believe in fairies! You might get your papa to hire men to watch in all the chimneys on Christmas Eve to catch Santa Claus, but even if they did not see Santa Claus coming down, what would that prove? Nobody sees Santa Claus, but that is no sign that there is no Santa Claus. The most real things in the world are those that neither children nor men can see. ... No Santa Claus! Thank God he lives, and he lives forever. A thousand years from now, Virginia, nay, ten times ten thousand years from now, he will continue to make glad the heart of childhood.

— FRANCIS P. CHURCH

the Merrie Christmas Days

Charts: Stockings for Good Little Girls and Boys, page 84;
Olde Toy Ornaments and Olde Toy Tree Skirt, page 85

Toyland, Toyland
Little girl and boy-land
While you dwell within it
You are ever happy then.

— *GLEN MAC DONOUGH*

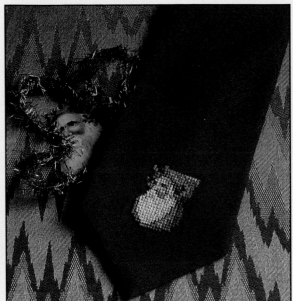

*S*ing hey! Sing hey!
For Christmas Day;
Twine mistletoe and holly.
For friendship glows
In winter snows,
And so let's all be jolly.

Charts: Christmas Album, page 86;
Angel Brooch, page 87;
Christmas Bag, page 89;
Santa Tie, page 88

Happy Christmas to all, and to all a good-night!

— *SANTA CLAUS*

Charts: Holiday Basket, page 91; Father Christmas Figure, page 92;
Winter Warmer for Her and Winter Warmer for Him, page 90;
Christmas Train Pajamas and Snowbunny Gown, page 88

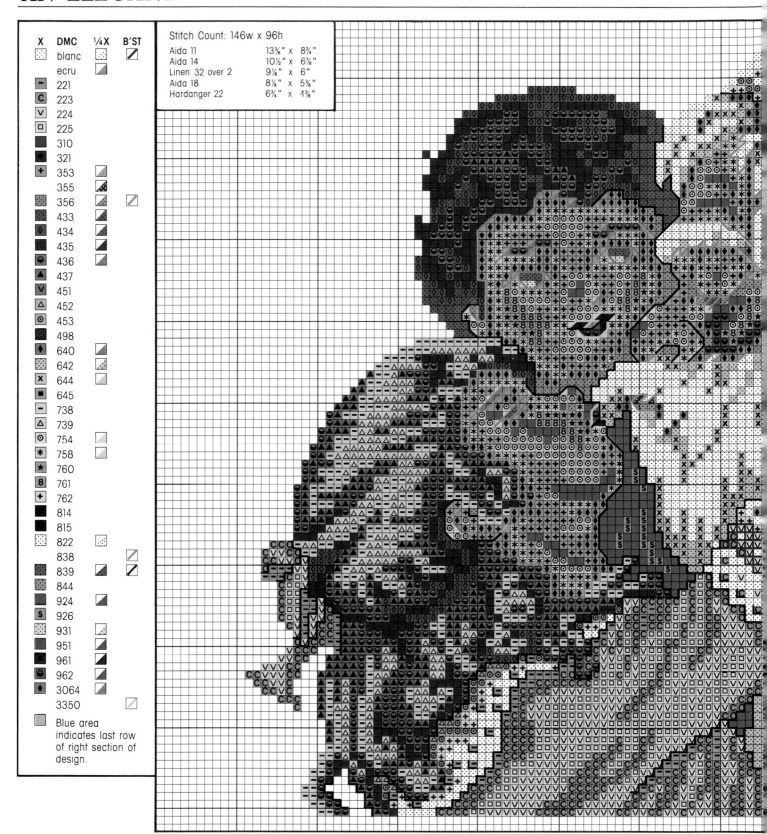

X	DMC	¼X	B'ST
⋰	blanc	⋰	
	ecru		◹
−	221		
C	223		
V	224		
□	225		
■	310		
✳	321		
✚	353		◹
	355	◪	
▦	356	◪	◹
▨	433	◪	
◆	434	◪	
▩	435	◪	
◓	436	◪	
▲	437		
V	451		
△	452		
⊙	453		
▥	498		
◆	640	◪	
▦	642	◪	
✕	644	◹	
■	645		
−	738		
△	739		
⊙	754	◹	
✳	758	◹	
★	760		
8	761		
✚	762		
■	814		
■	815		
⋰	822	⋰	
	838		◹
▨	839	◪	◹
	844	◹	
▦	924	◹	
S	926		
▦	931	◪	
▨	951	◹	
■	961	◹	
◉	962	◹	
◆	3064	◹	
	3350		◹

☐ Blue area indicates last row of right section of design.

Stitch Count: 146w x 96h

Aida 11	13⅜" x	8¾"
Aida 14	10½" x	6⅞"
Linen 32 over 2	9⅛" x	6"
Aida 18	8⅛" x	5⅜"
Hardanger 22	6¾" x	4⅜"

Kissing Santa in Frame (shown on pages 6-7): The design was stitched over 2 fabric threads on an 18" x 14" piece of Cream Belfast Linen (32 ct). Two strands of floss were used for Cross Stitch and 1 for Backstitch. It was custom framed.

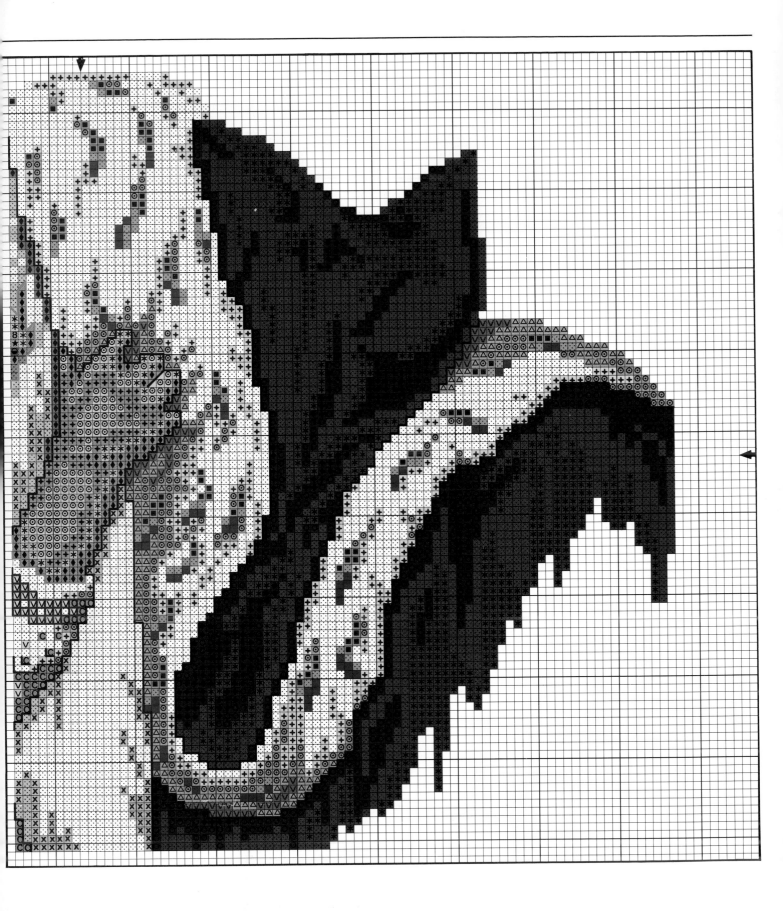

AN ELEGANT ERA

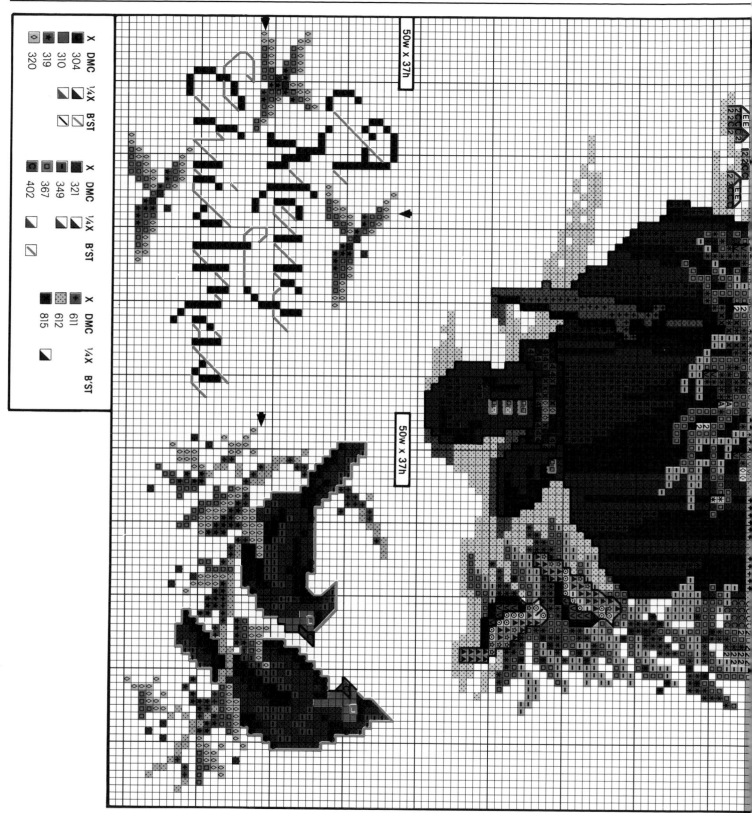

◇	★	▨	▪	X
				DMC
				304
				310
				319
				320

◨	◪	¼X
◱	◪	B'ST

◧	▨	✶	X
			DMC
			321
			349
			367
			402

| ◨ | ◨ | ◱ | ¼X |
| | | ◱ | B'ST |

■	▨	✷	X
			DMC
			611
			612
			815

| ◤ | ¼X |
| | B'ST |

50w x 37h

50w x 37h

Christmas Guest Towels (shown on page 12): Each design was centered and stitched over 2 fabric threads on a 12" x 20" piece of Cream Belfast Linen (32 ct), with bottom of each design 2¾" from one short edge of fabric. Two strands of floss were used for Cross Stitch and 1 for Backstitch. They were made into towels.

To finish each towel, press all edges ⅜" to wrong side. Press under ⅜" again and hem. Whipstitch a length of ¾"w lace to lower edge of towel.

Crimson Santa in Frame (shown on page 13): The design was stitched over 2 fabric threads on a 15" x 19" piece of Tea-Dyed Irish Linen (28 ct). Three strands of floss were used for Cross Stitch, 1 for Half Cross Stitch, and 1 for Backstitch. It was custom framed.

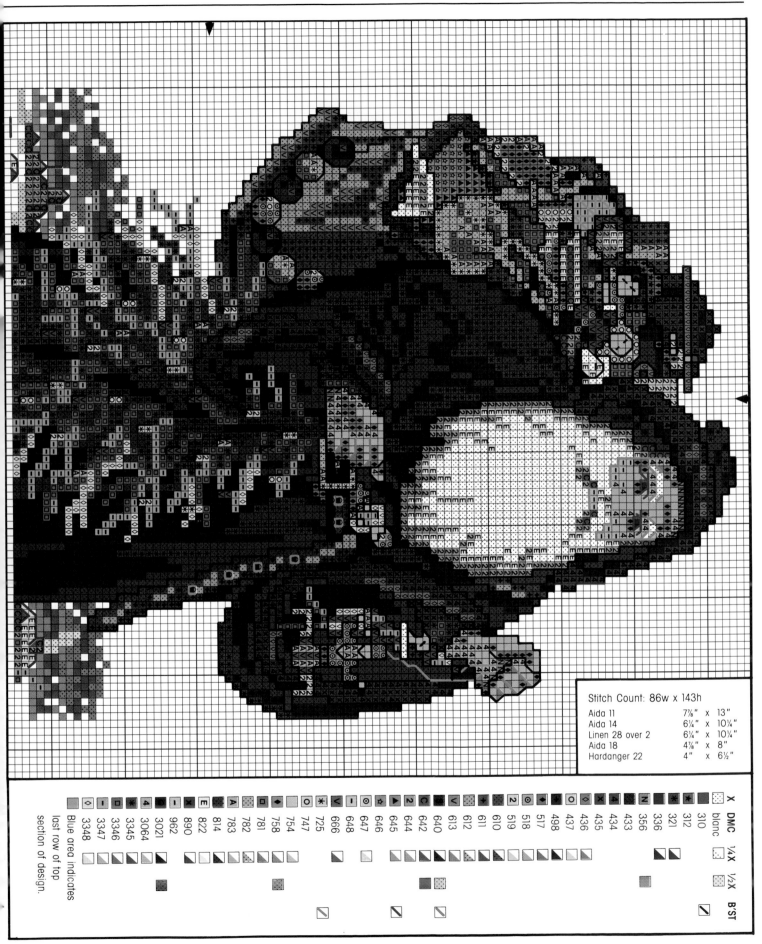

Stitch Count: 86w x 143h

Aida 11	7⅞"	x 13"
Aida 14	6¼"	x 10¼"
Linen 28 over 2	6¼"	x 10¼"
Aida 18	4⅞"	x 8"
Hardanger 22	4"	x 6½"

Blue area indicates
last row of top
section of design.

AN ELEGANT ERA

Christmas Tree Pillow (shown on page 12): The design was stitched over 2 fabric threads on a 10" square of Cream Belfast Linen (32 ct). Two strands of floss were used for Cross Stitch, 4 for metallic Cross Stitch, 1 for Half Cross Stitch, 2 for metallic Backstitch, and 1 for all other Backstitch. It was made into a pillow.

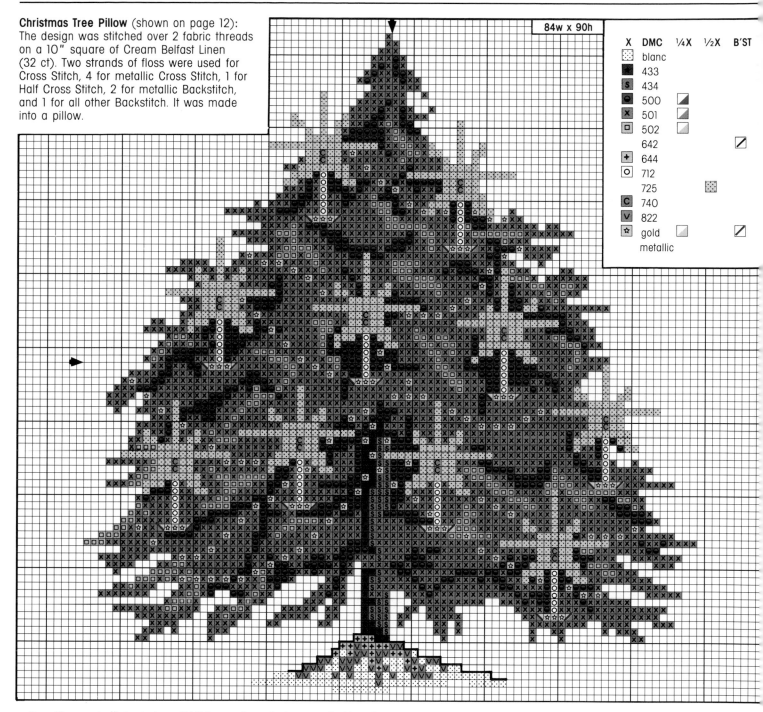

84w x 90h

X	DMC	¼X	½X	B'ST
∷	blanc			
■	433			
S	434			
⊙	500	◪		
⊠	501	◪		
▫	502	◪		
	642			◥
+	644			
○	712			
	725		▨	
C	740			
V	822			
☆	gold metallic	◪		◥

For pillow, cut stitched piece 1½" larger than design on all sides. Cut one piece of coordinating fabric same size as stitched piece for backing. Cut one piece of off-white fabric same size as stitched piece for lining.

With wrong sides facing and matching raw edges, baste stitched piece and lining together close to raw edges.

For cording, cut one 2" x 31" bias strip of coordinating fabric. Lay purchased cord along center of strip on wrong side of fabric; matching raw edges, fold strip over cord. Using zipper foot, baste along length of strip close to cord; trim seam allowance to ½". With seamlines matched, baste a 31" length of prefinished gold cording to top of fabric cording. With gold cording facing right side of stitched piece and raw edges matched, pin cording to stitched piece beginning at bottom edge of stitched piece and 1" from end of cording. Clip seam allowance of cording at corners. Using a ½" seam allowance, baste cording to stitched piece, ending basting 1" from opposite end of cording.

Open ends of fabric cording and cut cord so that ends meet. Fold fabric around cord. Overlap cording, turn ends toward raw edge of stitched piece, and use a ½" seam allowance to finish basting cording in place.

For lace ruffle, gather an 80" length of 2"w flat lace to fit stitched piece. Matching edges and beginning at bottom center of stitched piece, use a ½" seam allowance to sew lace to right side of stitched piece.

For fabric ruffle, fold short ends of a 5" x 80" length of coordinating fabric (pieced as necessary) ½" to wrong side. Fold strip in half lengthwise with wrong sides together and press. Gather fabric strip to fit stitched piece. Matching raw edges and beginning at one edge of stitched piece, use a ½" seam allowance to sew ruffle to right side of stitched piece.

With right sides facing and leaving an opening for turning, use a ½" seam allowance to sew stitched piece and backing fabric together; clip seam allowance at corners. Turn pillow right side out, carefully pushing corners outward. Stuff pillow with fiberfill and sew final closure by hand.

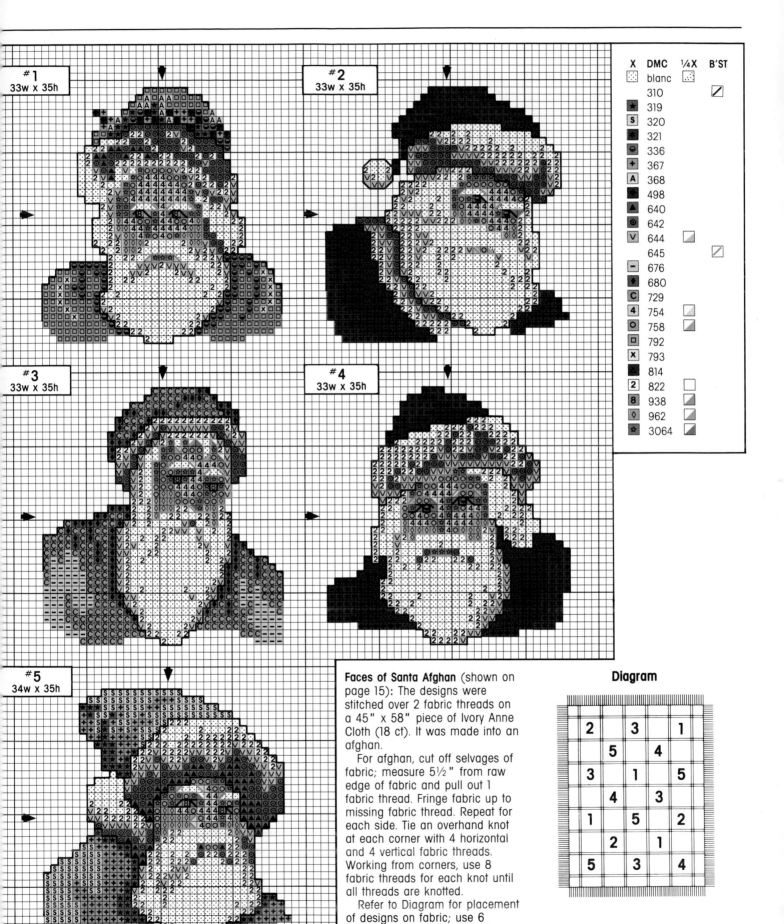

X	DMC	¼X	B'ST
⊡	blanc	⊡	
	310		◪
★	319		
S	320		
✳	321		
⊙	336		
✛	367		
A	368		
▲	498		
▲	640		
◉	642		
V	644	◰	
	645		◪
-	676		
◆	680		
C	729		
4	754	◰	
O	758	◰	
▢	792		
X	793		
▪	814		
2	822	▢	
8	938	◰	
◇	962	◰	
✦	3064	◰	

#1
33w x 35h

#2
33w x 35h

#3
33w x 35h

#4
33w x 35h

#5
34w x 35h

Faces of Santa Afghan (shown on page 15): The designs were stitched over 2 fabric threads on a 45" x 58" piece of Ivory Anne Cloth (18 ct). It was made into an afghan.

For afghan, cut off selvages of fabric; measure 5½" from raw edge of fabric and pull out 1 fabric thread. Fringe fabric up to missing fabric thread. Repeat for each side. Tie an overhand knot at each corner with 4 horizontal and 4 vertical fabric threads. Working from corners, use 8 fabric threads for each knot until all threads are knotted.

Refer to Diagram for placement of designs on fabric; use 6 strands of floss for Cross Stitch and 2 for Backstitch.

Diagram

2	3	1
	5	4	
3	1	5
	4	3	
1	5	2
	2	1	
5	3	4

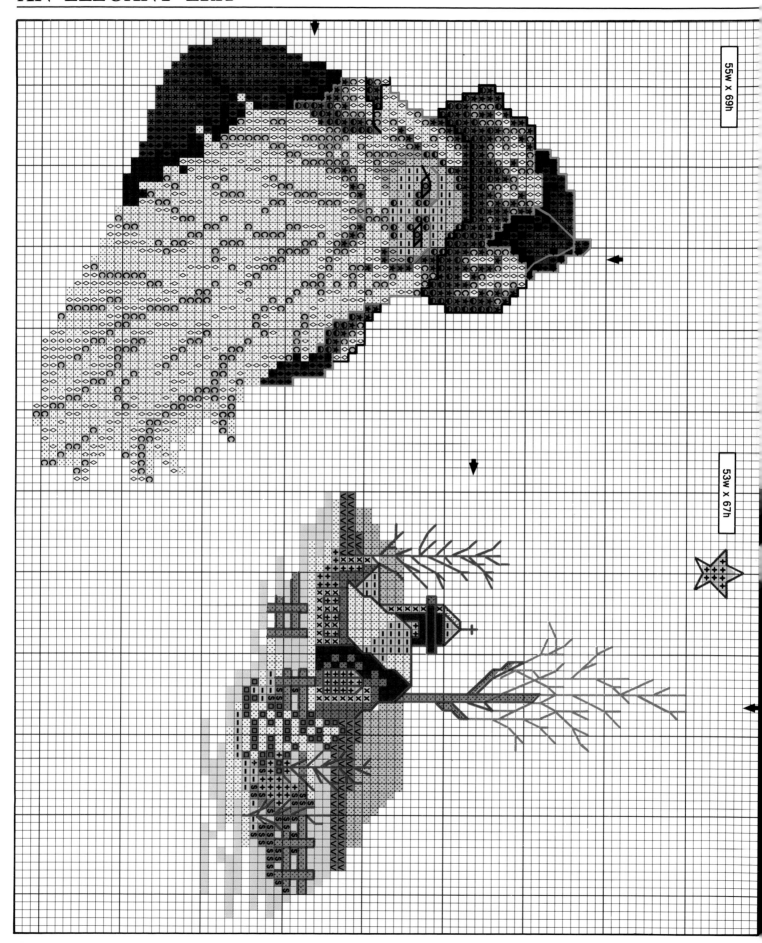

55w x 69h

53w x 67h

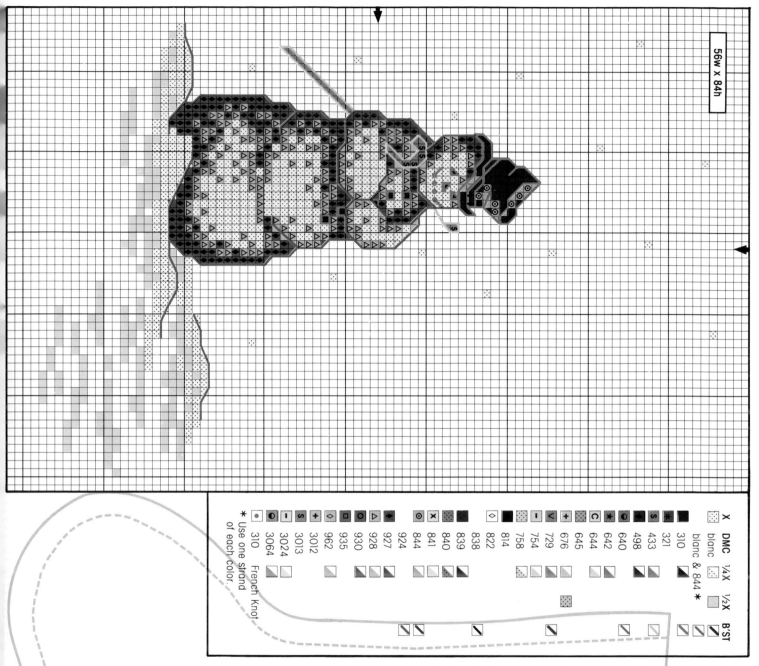

56w x 84h

X DMC 1/4X 1/2X B'ST
blanc
blanc & 844 ✱
310
321
433
498
640
642
644
645
676
729
754
758
814
822
838
839
840
841
844
924
927
928
930
935
962
3012
3013
3024
3064
310 French Knot

✱ Use one strand of each color.

Mini Stockings (shown on page 8): Each design was centered and stitched over 2 fabric threads on an 8" x 10" piece of Raw Belfast Linen (32 ct). Two strands of floss were used for Cross Stitch, 1 for Half Cross Stitch, 1 for Backstitch, and 1 for French Knots. They were made into mini stockings.

For each mini stocking, cut one 8" x 10" piece of Raw Belfast Linen for backing. Cut two 8" x 10" pieces of coordinating fabric for lining.

Trace stocking pattern onto tracing paper; cut out pattern. With right sides facing and matching raw edges, place stitched piece and backing fabric together. Place pattern on wrong side of stitched piece. Refer to photo to position design between stitching lines on pattern; pin pattern in place. Use fabric marking pencil to draw around pattern. Cutting through both layers, cut out stocking pieces. Repeat for lining pieces, cutting just inside drawn line.

For cording, cut one 2" x 18" bias strip of coordinating fabric. Lay purchased cord along center of strip on wrong side of fabric; matching raw edges, fold strip over cord. Using zipper foot, baste along length of strip close to cord; trim seam allowance to 1/4". Matching raw edges and beginning at one top corner, baste cording to right side of stitched piece. Continue around stitched piece to opposite top corner. Clip seam allowance at curves. Trim away excess cording.

With right sides facing and matching raw edges, pin stitched piece and backing fabric together. Using a 1/4" seam allowance and leaving top edge open, sew pieces together; clip seam allowance at curves. Turn stocking right side out. Press top edge 1/2" to wrong side.

With right sides facing and matching raw edges, pin lining pieces together. Using a 1/4" seam allowance and leaving top edge open, sew pieces together; clip seam allowance at curves. **Do not turn lining right side out.** Press top edge 1/2" to wrong side.

For hanger, cut one 1" x 3 1/2" strip of Raw Belfast Linen. Press each long edge of strip 1/4" to center. Matching long edges, fold strip in half and sew close to folded edges. Matching short edges, fold hanger in half and whipstitch to inside of stocking at left seam.

With wrong sides facing, place lining inside stocking. Matching pressed edge of lining to pressed edge of stocking, whipstitch lining to stocking.

AN ELEGANT ERA

Porcelain Jars (shown on page 9): Each design was stitched over 2 fabric threads on an 8" square of Cream Belfast Linen (32 ct). Two strands of floss were used for Cross Stitch, 1 for Backstitch, and 1 for French Knots. They were inserted in the lids of 5" dia. porcelain jars (4" dia. lid opening).

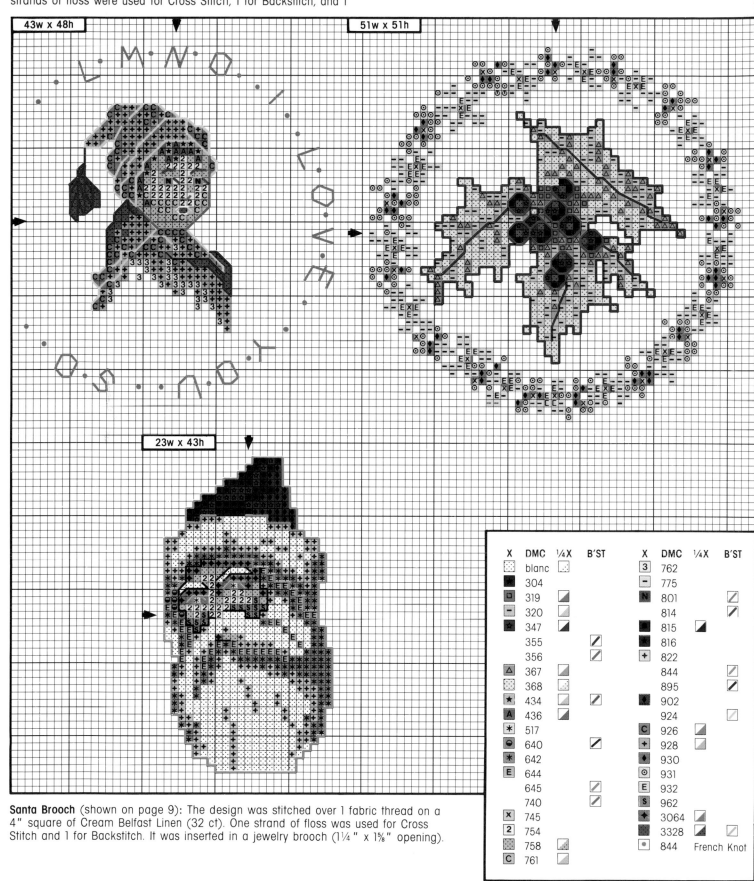

Santa Brooch (shown on page 9): The design was stitched over 1 fabric thread on a 4" square of Cream Belfast Linen (32 ct). One strand of floss was used for Cross Stitch and 1 for Backstitch. It was inserted in a jewelry brooch (1¼" x 1⅝" opening).

X	DMC	¼X	B'ST		X	DMC	¼X	B'ST
	blanc				3	762		
	304				-	775		
	319				N	801		
-	320					814		
	347					815		
	355					816		
	356				+	822		
	367					844		
	368					895		
	434					902		
A	436					924		
	517				C	926		
	640				+	928		
	642					930		
E	644					931		
	645				E	932		
	740				S	962		
X	745					3064		
2	754					3328		
	758					844	French Knot
C	761							

56

Christmas Card (shown on page 11): The design was centered and stitched over 2 fabric threads on a 4¾" x 6¾" piece of Cream Belfast Linen (32 ct). Two strands of floss were used for Cross Stitch and 1 for Backstitch. It was inserted in a Christmas card (3" x 5" opening).

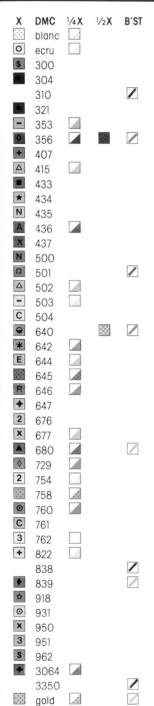

X	DMC	¼X	½X	B'ST
⌁	blanc	⌁		
O	ecru	▢		
S	300			
■	304			
	310			╱
✳	321			
–	353	◣		
◇	356	◣	◪	╱
✚	407			
△	415	◣		
■	433			
★	434			
N	435			
A	436	◣		
X	437			
N	500			
▢	501			╱
△	502	◣		
–	503	◣		
C	504			
⊙	640		▨	╱
✳	642	◣		
E	644	◣		
▨	645	◣		
R	646	◣		
✚	647			
2	676			
X	677	◣		
▲	680	◣		◪
◇	729	◣		
2	754	▢		
▨	758		◣	
⊙	760	◣		
C	761	▢		
3	762	▢		
✚	822	▢		
	838			╱
◆	839			◪
★	918			
⊙	931			
X	950	▢		
3	951			
S	962			
◆	3064	◣		
	3350			╱
▨	gold	◣		◪
	metallic			

23w x 47h

38w x 64h

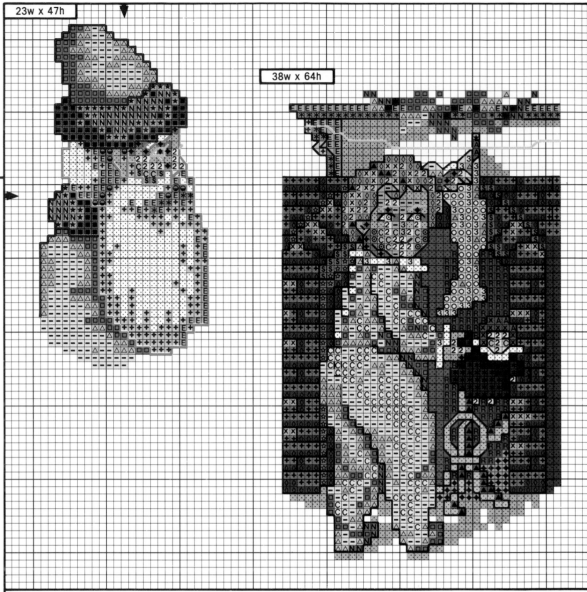

Ready for Santa Hanging Pillow (shown on page 11): The design was stitched over 2 fabric threads on a 9" x 11" piece of Cream Belfast Linen (32 ct). Two strands of floss were used for Cross Stitch, 1 for Half Cross Stitch, and 1 for Backstitch. It was made into a hanging pillow.

For hanging pillow, cut stitched piece 1½" larger than design on all sides. Cut one piece of coordinating fabric same size as stitched piece for backing. Cut one piece of off-white fabric same size as stitched piece for lining.

With wrong sides facing and matching raw edges, baste stitched piece and lining together close to raw edges.

For cording, cut one 2" x 24" bias strip of coordinating fabric. Lay purchased cord along center of strip on wrong side of fabric; matching raw edges, fold strip over cord. Using zipper foot, baste along length of strip close to cord; trim seam allowance to ½". Matching raw edges and beginning at bottom center, pin cording to right side of stitched piece. Ends of cording should overlap approximately 2"; pin overlapping end

out of the way.

Starting 2" from beginning end of cording, baste cording to stitched piece. Clip seam allowance at corners.

On overlapping end of cording, remove 2½" of basting; fold end of fabric back and trim cord so that it meets beginning end of cord. Fold end of fabric under ½"; wrap fabric over beginning end of cording. Finish basting cording to stitched piece.

For lace ruffle, gather a 42" length of 2"w flat lace to fit stitched piece. Matching edges and beginning at bottom center of stitched piece, use a ½" seam allowance to sew lace to right side of stitched piece.

With right sides facing and leaving an opening for turning, use a ½" seam allowance to sew stitched piece and backing fabric together; clip seam allowance at corners. Turn pillow right side out, carefully pushing corners outward. Stuff pillow with polyester fiberfill and sew final closure by hand.

For hanger, cut two 18" lengths of ⅜"w ribbon. Whipstitch one end of each length to one top corner of pillow at seam.

AN ELEGANT ERA

41w x 41h

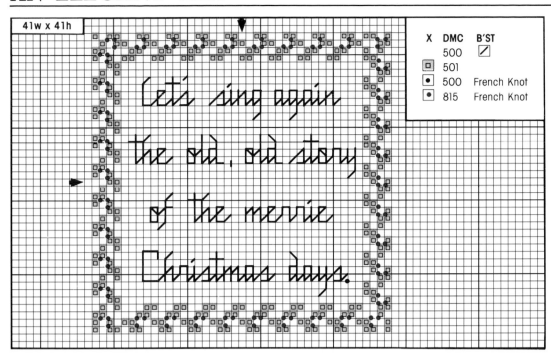

X	DMC	B'ST
	500	◪
▣	501	
•	500	French Knot
●	815	French Knot

Memory Box (shown on page 10): The design was stitched over 2 fabric threads on an 8" square of Cream Belfast Linen (32 ct). Two strands of floss were used for Cross Stitch, 1 for Backstitch, and 1 for French Knots. It was inserted in a small collector's cabinet (3½" square opening).

78w x 35h

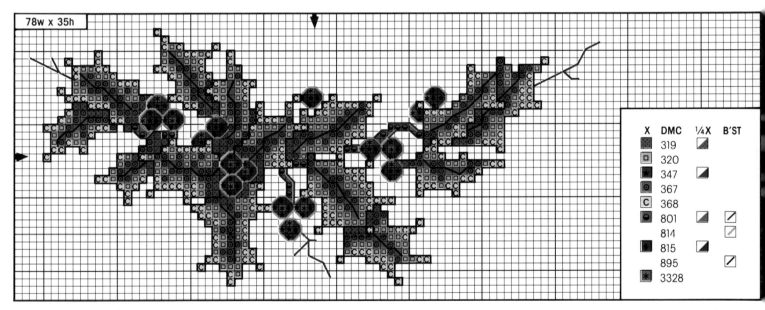

X	DMC	¼X	B'ST
▦	319	◪	
▣	320		
◼	347	◪	
◉	367		
C	368		
◒	801	◪	◪
	814		◪
◼	815	◪	
	895		◪
✳	3328		

Mini Tree Skirt (shown on page 19): The design was centered and stitched over 2 fabric threads on a 20" square of Cream Belfast Linen (32 ct), with bottom of design 2" from one edge of fabric. Two strands of floss were used for Cross Stitch and 1 for Backstitch. It was made into a mini tree skirt.

For mini tree skirt, cut one 20" square of off-white fabric for backing. Fold fabric in half from top to bottom and again from left to right. To mark outer cutting line, tie one end of a 12" length of string to a fabric marking pencil. Insert a thumbtack through string 9" from pencil. Insert thumbtack in fabric as shown in **Fig. 1** and mark one-fourth of a circle.

To mark inner cutting line, insert thumbtack through string ¾" from pencil

and mark one-fourth of a circle. Following cutting lines and cutting through all thicknesses, cut out backing piece. For slit in back of skirt, cut along one fold from outer edge to inner edge.

Referring to photo for placement of design, place backing piece on wrong side of stitched piece with bottom of design 1¼" from outer edge of backing. Use fabric marking pencil to draw around all cut edges of backing. Cut out stitched piece.

For cording, cut one 2" x 60" bias strip of coordinating fabric (pieced as necessary). Lay purchased cord along center of strip on wrong side of fabric; matching raw edges, fold strip over cord. Using zipper foot, baste along length of strip close to cord; trim seam allowance to ½". Matching raw edges, begin at one back corner and baste

cording to right side of outer edge of stitched piece. Clip seam allowance at curves. Trim away excess cording.

With right sides facing and matching raw edges, pin stitched piece and backing fabric together. Using a ½" seam allowance and leaving one straight edge open, sew pieces together; clip seam allowance at curves. Turn tree skirt right side out and press. Sew final closure by hand.

Fig. 1

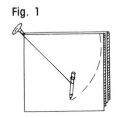

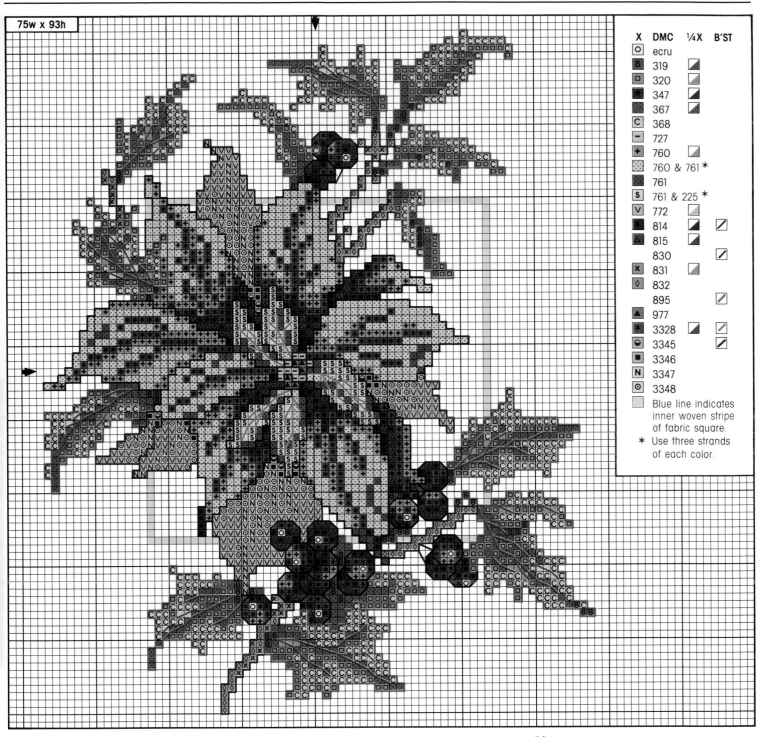

75w x 93h

X	DMC	¼X	B'ST
O	ecru		
8	319	◢	
□	320	◢	
◼	347	◢	
▦	367	◢	
C	368		
-	727		
+	760	◢	
⋯	760 & 761 *		
■	761		
S	761 & 225 *		
V	772	◢	
◼	814	◢	◸
▲	815	◢	
	830		◸
X	831	◢	
◇	832	◢	
	895		◸
▲	977		◸
✳	3328	◢	◸
⊙	3345		◸
■	3346		
N	3347		
⊙	3348		
▨	Blue line indicates inner woven stripe of fabric square.		
*	Use three strands of each color.		

Poinsettia Afghan (shown on page 25): The design was stitched over 2 fabric threads on a 45" x 58" piece of Ivory Anne Cloth (18 ct). It was made into an afghan.

For afghan, cut off selvages of fabric; measure 5½" from raw edge of fabric and pull out 1 fabric thread. Fringe fabric up to missing fabric thread. Repeat for each side. Tie an overhand knot at each corner with 4 horizontal and 4 vertical fabric threads. Working from corners, use 8 fabric threads for each knot until all threads are knotted.

Refer to Diagram for placement of design on fabric; use 6 strands of floss for Cross Stitch and 2 for Backstitch.

Diagram

AN ELEGANT ERA

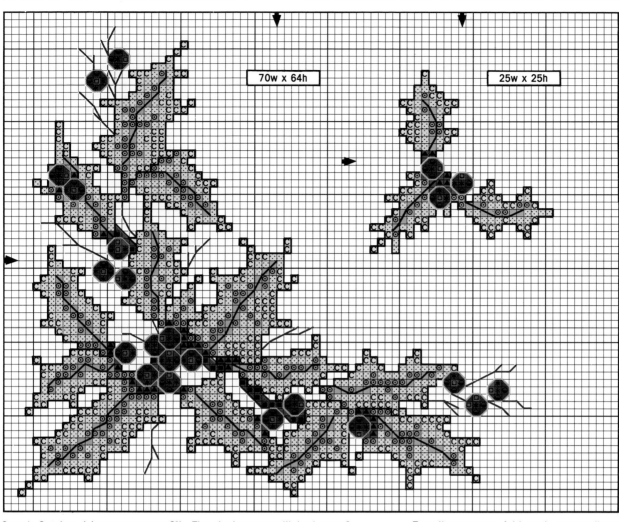

70w x 64h

25w x 25h

X	DMC	¼X	B'ST
▲	319	◢	
⊡	320	⊡	
✳	347	◢	
⊙	367	◢	
C	368		
◼	801	◢	◢
	814	◢	◢
◼	815	◢	
	895		◢
◼	3328	◢	

Napkin (shown on page 20): The design was stitched over 2 fabric threads on a 14¾" square napkin. For napkin, cut a 16" square of Cream Belfast Linen (32 ct). Refer to Double Hemstitch instructions to hem edges of fabric. Center and stitch design in one corner of napkin, with edges of design 1⅛" from edges of fabric. Use 2 strands of floss for Cross Stitch and 1 for Backstitch.

Crumb Catcher (shown on page 21): The design was stitched over 2 fabric threads on a 32" square crumb catcher. For crumb catcher, cut a 34" square of Cream Belfast Linen (32 ct). Refer to Double Hemstitch instructions to hem edges of fabric. Center and stitch design in one corner of crumb catcher, with edges of design 2" from edges of fabric. Use 2 strands of floss for Cross Stitch and 1 for Backstitch.

Double Hemstitch Instructions

Note: Measurements in instructions are for edges of crumb catcher; refer to measurements in parentheses for edges of napkin.

To hemstitch fabric pieces, measure 1¾" (1") from one raw edge and pull out one fabric thread. Working toward center of fabric, withdraw fabric threads for ⅛"; repeat for each edge. Fold one edge of fabric 1" (⅝") to wrong side; press and unfold. Repeat for each edge.

To miter corners, fold each corner diagonally to the wrong side until fold lines on right and wrong sides of fabric (dashed and solid lines of **Fig. 1**) are matched. Trim off corner ¼" from folded edge. Fold remaining raw edges ¼" to wrong side; press. Following first fold lines and mitering corners (**Fig. 2**), fold hem ¾" (⅜") to wrong side and pin in place; folded edge of hem should be at edge of withdrawn area.

Secure one strand of ecru floss at a corner of fabric on wrong side. Bring needle under 4 fabric threads in the withdrawn area (**Fig. 3**). Bring needle under same fabric threads a second time and come up with needle through edge of fold (**Fig. 4**); firmly pull on thread. Bring needle under same number of fabric threads for each stitch, continue until fabric is hemmed. Turn fabric and repeat to work hemstitch around inside edge of withdrawn area (**Fig. 5**).

Fig. 1

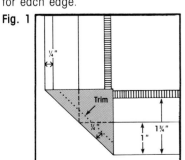

Fig. 2

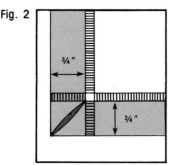

Fig. 3

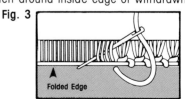

Fig. 4

Fig. 5

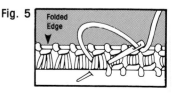

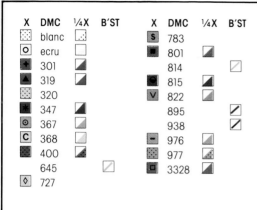

X	DMC	¼X	B'ST	X	DMC	¼X	B'ST
∷	blanc			S	783	◤	
o	ecru			■	801	◤	
+	301	◤			814		◹
▲	319	◤			815	◤	
▦	320			V	822	◤	
★	347	◤			895		◸
◉	367	◤			938		◸
C	368	◤		-	976	◤	
▨	400	◤		∷	977	◤	
	645		◹	▣	3328	◤	
◇	727						

Heart String (shown on page 22): The design was stitched over 2 fabric threads on a 7" square of Cream Belfast Linen (32 ct). Two strands of floss were used for Cross Stitch and 1 for Backstitch. It was made into a heart string.

For large heart, cut one 7" square of coordinating fabric for backing.

Fold tracing paper in half and match fold to dashed line of large heart pattern. Trace large heart pattern onto folded tracing paper; leaving paper folded, cut out pattern. Unfold pattern and press to flatten. With right sides facing and matching raw edges, place stitched piece and backing fabric together. Center pattern on wrong side of stitched piece. Use fabric marking pencil to draw around pattern. Cut out fabric pieces.

For cording, cut one 2" x 18" bias strip of coordinating fabric. Lay purchased cord along center of strip on wrong side of fabric; matching raw edges, fold strip over cord. Using zipper foot, baste along length of strip close to cord; trim seam allowance to ¼". Matching raw edges and beginning at one side, pin cording to right side of stitched piece. Ends of cording should overlap approximately 2"; pin overlapping end out of the way. Starting 2" from beginning end of cording, baste cording to stitched piece. Clip seam allowance at curves.

On overlapping end of cording, remove 2½" of basting; fold end of fabric back and trim cord so that it meets beginning end of cord. Fold end of fabric under ½"; wrap fabric over beginning end of cording. Finish basting cording to stitched piece.

With right sides facing and matching raw edges, pin stitched piece and backing fabric together. Using a ¼" seam allowance and leaving an opening for turning, sew pieces together; clip seam allowance at curves. Turn heart right side out. Stuff heart with polyester fiberfill and sew final closure by hand.

For small hearts, cut four 5" squares of coordinating fabric. Using small heart pattern and 12" lengths of cording, repeat large heart instructions to make two small hearts.

For heart string, refer to photo and whipstitch hearts together. Cut two 42" lengths of ¼"w ribbon and fold each length in half. Whipstitch fold of one length of ribbon to each end of heart string.

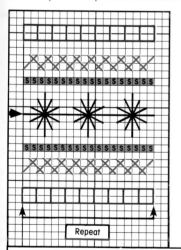

X	COLOR	STITCH
◹	gold metallic	Four Sided Stitch
◹	DMC 498 or 501	Herringbone Stitch
S	gold metallic	Cross Stitch
◹	gold metallic	Algerian Eye Stitch

Christmas Crackers (shown on page 23): The design was stitched using DMC 501 on a 7" length of Seafoam Green/Ivory Ribband® II (14 ct). The design was stitched using DMC 498 on a 7" length of Burgundy/Ivory Ribband® II (14 ct). The design was repeated along Ribband® lengths. Two strands of floss were used for Herringbone Stitches and 2 strands of gold metallic thread were used for Algerian Eye Stitches, Cross Stitches, and Four-Sided Stitches. (See Stitch Diagrams, page 94). They were made into Christmas crackers.

For each Christmas cracker, cut one 15" x 6½" piece of fabric. Press each long edge of fabric ½" to wrong side and each short edge 2" to wrong side; use fabric glue stick to glue edges to wrong side of fabric.

Fig. 1

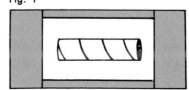

Insert candy or small gift in a 5" length of 1½" dia. cardboard tube. Center tube lengthwise on wrong side of fabric (**Fig. 1**). Fold long edges of fabric around tube and use fabric glue stick to glue fabric edges together along length of tube only.

Cut two 18" lengths of gold cord. Tie fabric at ends of tube with lengths of cord.

For gold band around wrapper, cut one 6½" square of gold lamé fabric. Fold lamé in half matching raw edges; use a ½" seam allowance to sew along edge opposite fold. Turn band right side out; with seam centered, press band flat. With seam down, center and wrap band around cracker; fold top edge under ½" and whipstitch short edges of band together.

Center Ribband® over gold band; fold top edge under ½" and whipstitch short edges of Ribband® together.

AN ELEGANT ERA

X	DMC
■	304
V	501
◉	640

Nosegay Place Card (shown on page 20): A letter from the alphabet was centered and stitched on a 6" square of Natural perforated paper (14 ct). Three strands of floss were used for Cross Stitch. (See Working on Perforated Paper, page 95.) It was made into a place card.

For place card, trace Heart pattern onto tracing paper; cut out pattern. Center pattern on wrong side of stitched piece and draw around pattern. Cut out heart.

Cut one 8¾" length of ½"w pregathered lace. Refer to photo to glue gathered edge of lace to wrong side of heart; allow glue to dry.

Cut one 18" length of ¹⁄₁₆"w ribbon. Refer to x's on pattern to thread ribbon ends from back to front of heart through holes in paper. Insert a small nosegay of holly into ribbon loop at back of heart; tie ribbon in a bow at front of heart.

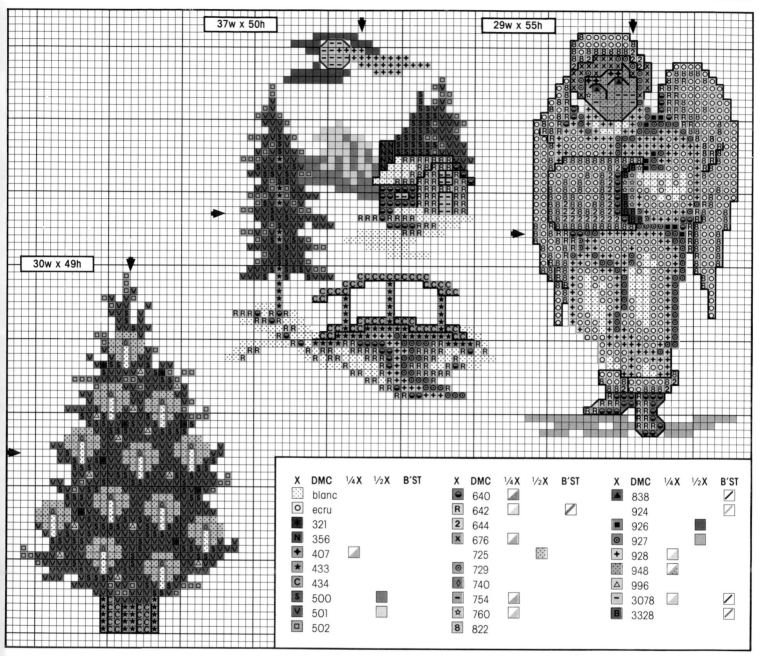

X	DMC	1/4X	1/2X	B'ST		X	DMC	1/4X	1/2X	B'ST		X	DMC	1/4X	1/2X	B'ST
	blanc					⊖	640	◪				▲	838			◪
○	ecru					R	642	◪		◪			924			◪
✱	321					2	644					◼	926		◼	
N	356					X	676	◪				⊙	927		◼	
◆	407	◪					725		▦			+	928	◪		
★	433					⊙	729						948	◪		
C	434					◇	740					△	996			
S	500		◼			-	754	◪				-	3078	◪		◪
V	501		◻			☆	760	◪				B	3328			◪
◻	502					8	822									

Labels on pattern: 37w x 50h, 29w x 55h, 30w x 49h

Bell Ornaments (shown on page 17): Each design was stitched over 2 fabric threads on a 6" x 8½" piece of Cream Belfast Linen (32 ct). Two strands of floss were used for Cross Stitch, 1 for Half Cross Stitch, and 1 for Backstitch. They were made into ornaments.

For each ornament, cut two 6" x 7" pieces of coordinating fabric; cut one 6" x 8½" piece of medium weight fusible interfacing. Follow manufacturer's instructions to fuse interfacing to wrong side of stitched piece.

For first bell pattern, place tracing paper over bell pattern, page 95, and trace solid black and grey lines only onto tracing paper; cut out pattern. Center pattern on a 6" x 7" piece of lightweight cardboard and draw around pattern; cut out bell shape. Center cardboard bell on wrong side of one coordinating fabric piece and use a fabric marking pencil to draw around bell shape. Leaving ½" around drawn line, cut out fabric bell.

Center cardboard bell on wrong side of fabric bell, matching edge of cardboard to drawn line on fabric. At approx. ¼" intervals, clip edge of fabric to within ⅛" of drawn line. Pulling fabric taut, glue edges of fabric to back of cardboard bell.

For second bell pattern, follow instructions for first bell pattern, tracing grey and dashed lines only of bell pattern; cut out pattern. With bottom of design approximately ¾" from bottom of pattern, place pattern on stitched piece. Use fabric marking pencil to draw around pattern; cut out stitched piece. Apply a thin layer of glue to wrong side of stitched piece. Matching top edges, glue stitched piece to front of bell; glue bottom edge of stitched piece to wrong side of bell.

With ends of cord extending ½" past bottom of stitched piece, refer to photo to glue one 14" length of gold cord over raw edges of stitched piece; glue ends of cord to wrong side of bell.

For clapper, cut three 6" lengths of gold cord. Knot lengths together in center; trim ends to 1". Referring to photo, center and glue cord to wrong side of bell.

For hanger, cut one 8" length of gold cord. Fold cord in half and glue ends to top center of bell on wrong side.

For backing, use first bell pattern. Center pattern on remaining fabric piece and draw around pattern. Cutting ⅛" inside drawn line, cut out remaining fabric bell. With wrong sides facing, glue backing piece to bell.

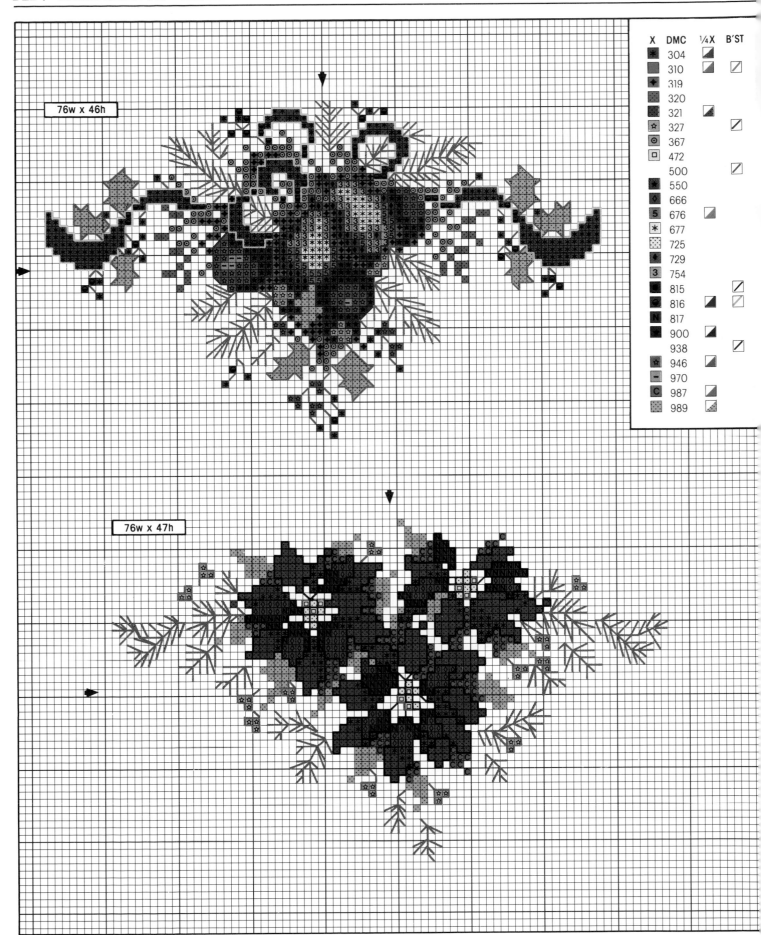

76w x 46h

76w x 47h

X	DMC	¼X	B'ST
✹	304	◤	
	310	◤	◢
◆	319		
	320		
	321	◤	◢
☆	327		◢
⊙	367		
▢	472		◢
	500		◢
✹	550		
◊	666		
5	676	◤	
✳	677		
⋰	725		
◆	729		
3	754		
■	815		◢
◒	816	◤	◢
N	817		
◼	900	◤	◢
	938		
☆	946	◤	
–	970		
C	987	◤	
⋰	989	◤	

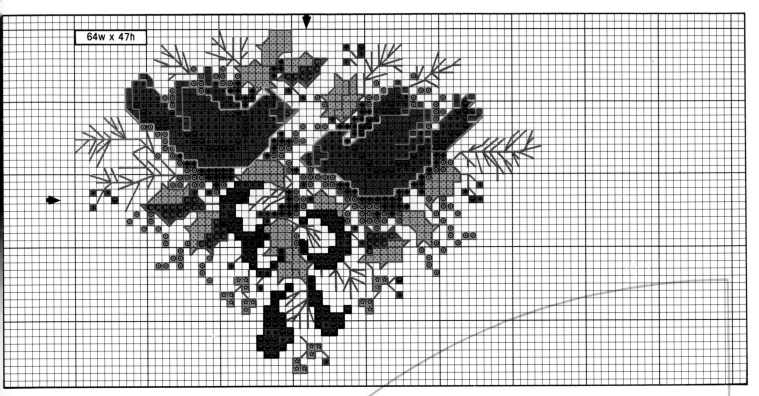

64w x 47h

Victorian Cornucopias (shown on page 16): Each design was stitched on a 12" x 10" piece of Ivory Aida (18 ct). Two strands of floss were used for Cross Stitch and 1 for Backstitch. They were made into cornucopia ornaments.

For each ornament, cut one 12" x 10" piece of lightweight fusible interfacing. Cut one 12" x 10" piece of coordinating fabric for lining. Follow manufacturer's instructions to fuse interfacing to wrong side of lining fabric.

Trace cornucopia pattern onto tracing paper; cut out pattern. With right sides facing and matching raw edges, pin stitched piece and lining fabric together. Center pattern on wrong side of stitched piece with bottom point of pattern 3" below bottom of design; use fabric marking pencil to draw around pattern. Cut out shapes.

With right side to the inside and matching straight edges, fold stitched piece in half. Use a ¼" seam allowance to sew along long edges. Turn fabric right side out.

With right side to the inside and matching straight edges, fold lining in half. Use a ¼" seam allowance to sew along long edges. **Do not turn lining right side out.** Press top edge of lining ¼" to wrong side.

For cording, cut one 2" x 12" bias strip of coordinating fabric. Lay purchased cord along center of strip on wrong side of fabric; matching raw edges, fold strip over cord. Using zipper foot, baste along length of strip close to cord; trim seam allowance to ¼". Matching raw edges and beginning at back seam, pin cording to right side of stitched piece. Ends of cording should overlap approximately 2"; pin overlapping end out of the way.

Starting 2" from beginning end of cording, baste cording to stitched piece.

On overlapping end of cording, remove 2½" of basting; fold end of fabric back and trim cord so that it meets beginning end of cord. Fold end of fabric under ½"; wrap fabric over beginning end of cording. Finish basting cording to stitched piece. Following basting lines, sew cording to stitched piece. Press top edge of stitched piece ¼" to wrong side.

With wrong sides facing and matching seams, insert lining

inside stitched piece. Whipstitch lining and stitched piece together around top edge.

For hanger, cut two 36" lengths of ¹⁄₁₆"w ribbon; fold each length in half. With seam of ornament centered at back, refer to photo to whipstitch fold of one length to right side of ornament; measure along ribbon 7" from fold and tack ribbon to left side of ornament. Tack fold of remaining length over ribbon at left side. Referring to photo, tie knots in ribbon lengths; trim ends of ribbon to uneven lengths.

Bottom Point

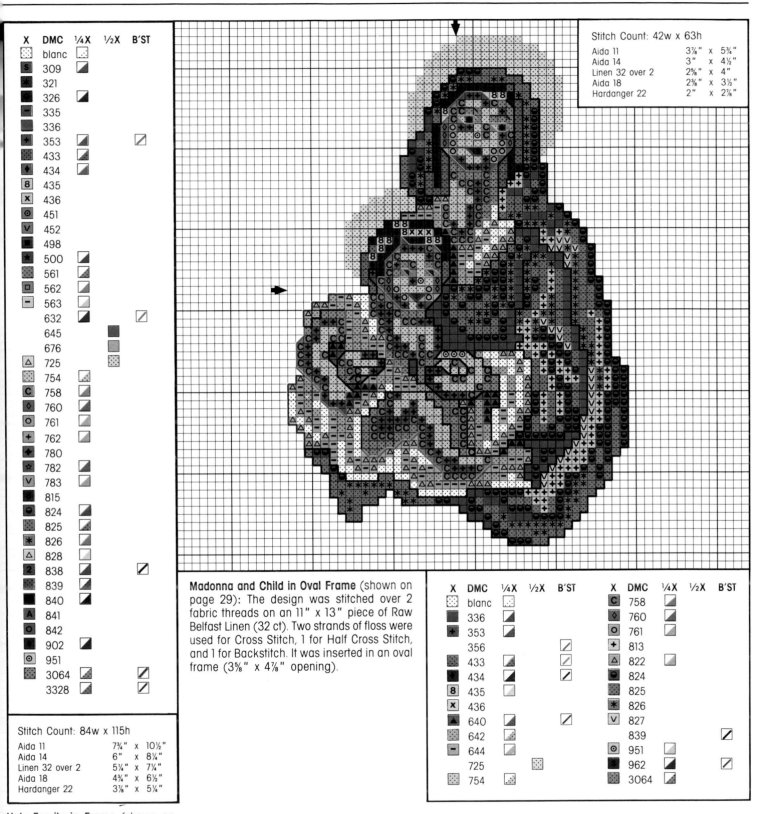

Stitch Count: 42w x 63h

Aida 11	3⅞" x 5¾"
Aida 14	3" x 4½"
Linen 32 over 2	2⅝" x 4"
Aida 18	2⅜" x 3½"
Hardanger 22	2" x 2⅞"

X	DMC	¼X	½X	B'ST
	blanc			
S	309	◪		
✳	321			
	326	◪		
–	335			
	336			
★	353	◪		◪
	433	◪		
◆	434	◪		
8	435			
X	436			
⊙	451			
V	452			
	498			
★	500	◪		
	561			
□	562			
–	563			
	632	◪		◪
	645	■		
	676	▨		
△	725	▨		
	754	▨		
C	758	◪		
◇	760	◪		
O	761	◪		
+	762	◪		
✦	780	◪		
☆	782	◪		
V	783	◪		
	815			
●	824	◪		
	825	◪		
✳	826			
△	828			
2	838	◪		◪
	839	◪		
	840	◪		
A	841			
⊙	842			
	902	◪		
⊙	951			
	3064	▨		◪
	3328	◪		◪

Stitch Count: 84w x 115h

Aida 11	7¾" x 10½"
Aida 14	6" x 8¼"
Linen 32 over 2	5¼" x 7¼"
Aida 18	4¾" x 6½"
Hardanger 22	3⅞" x 5¼"

Madonna and Child in Oval Frame (shown on page 29): The design was stitched over 2 fabric threads on an 11" x 13" piece of Raw Belfast Linen (32 ct). Two strands of floss were used for Cross Stitch, 1 for Half Cross Stitch, and 1 for Backstitch. It was inserted in an oval frame (3⅝" x 4⅞" opening).

X	DMC	¼X	½X	B'ST		X	DMC	¼X	½X	B'ST
▨	blanc	▨				C	758	◪		
■	336					◇	760	◪		
✦	353	◪				O	761	◪		
	356			◪		+	813	◪		
	433	◪		◪		△	822	◪		◪
	434	◪		◪		◉	824			
8	435	□					825			
X	436					✳	826			
▲	640	◪		◪		V	827			◪
	642	◪					839			◪
–	644	◪				⊙	951	□		
	725		▨				962	◪		◪
▨	754	▨					3064	◪		

Holy Family in Frame (shown on page 27): The design was stitched over 2 fabric threads on a 14" x 16" piece of Raw Belfast Linen (32 ct). Two strands of floss were used for Cross Stitch, 1 for Half Cross Stitch, and 1 for Backstitch. It was custom framed.

O COME, LET US ADORE HIM

Christmas Splendor Hanging Pillow (shown on page 32): The design was stitched over 2 fabric threads on a 16" x 11" piece of Tea-Dyed Irish Linen (28 ct). Three strands of floss were used for Cross Stitch, 2 for DMC 991 Backstitch, 1 for all other Backstitch, and 2 for French Knot. It was made into a hanging pillow.

For hanging pillow, cut stitched piece 1½" larger than design on all sides. Cut one piece of coordinating fabric same size as stitched piece for backing. Cut one piece of tan fabric same size as stitched piece for lining.

With wrong sides facing and matching raw edges, baste stitched piece and lining together close to raw edges.

For cording, cut one 2" x 31" bias strip of coordinating fabric. Lay purchased cord along center of strip on wrong side of fabric; matching raw edges, fold strip over cord. Using zipper foot, baste along length of strip close to cord; trim seam allowance to ½". Matching raw edges and beginning at bottom center, pin cording to right side of stitched piece. Ends of cording should overlap approximately 2"; pin overlapping end out of the way.

Starting 2" from beginning end of cording, baste cording to stitched piece. Clip seam allowance at corners.

On overlapping end of cording, remove 2½" of basting; fold end of fabric back and trim cord so that it meets beginning end of cord. Fold end of fabric under ½"; wrap fabric over beginning end of cording. Finish basting cording to stitched piece.

For lace ruffle, gather a 56" length of 2"w flat lace to fit stitched piece. Matching edges and beginning at bottom center of stitched piece, use a ½" seam allowance to sew lace to right side of stitched piece.

With right sides facing and leaving an opening for turning, use a ½" seam allowance to sew stitched piece and backing fabric together; clip seam allowance at corners. Turn pillow right side out, carefully pushing corners outward. Stuff pillow with polyester fiberfill and sew final closure by hand.

For hanger, cut two 34" lengths of ⅜"w ribbon. Whipstitch one end of each length to one top corner of pillow at seam.

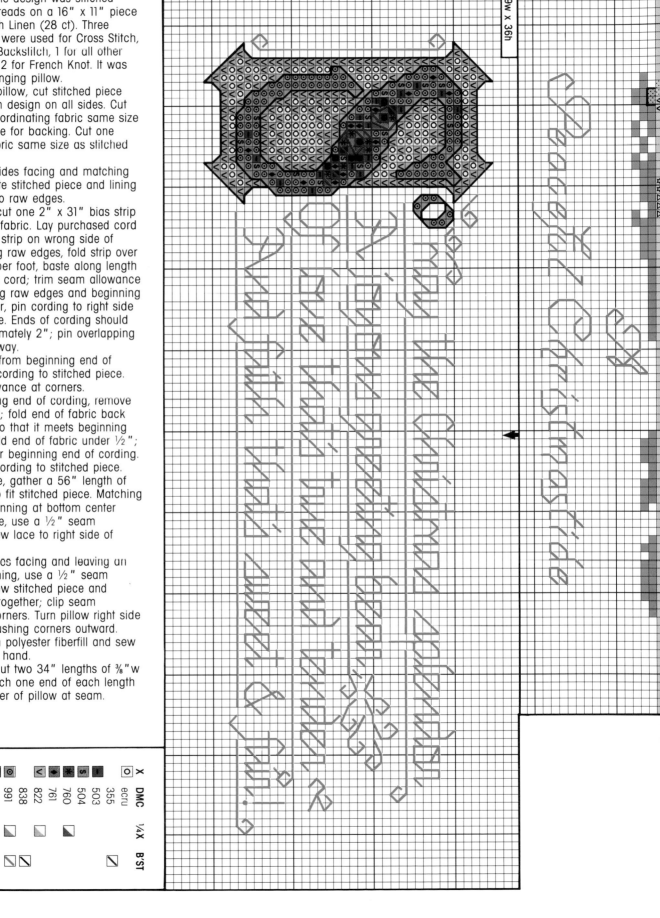

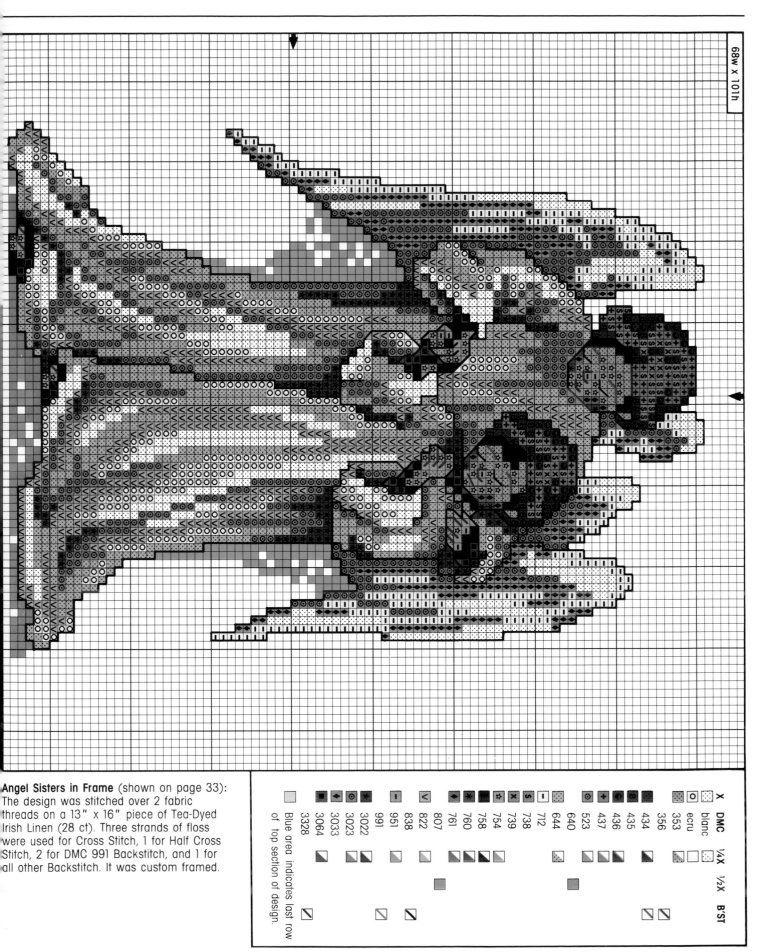

Angel Sisters in Frame (shown on page 33):
The design was stitched over 2 fabric
threads on a 13" x 16" piece of Tea-Dyed
Irish Linen (28 ct). Three strands of floss
were used for Cross Stitch, 1 for Half Cross
Stitch, 2 for DMC 991 Backstitch, and 1 for
all other Backstitch. It was custom framed.

O COME, LET US ADORE HIM

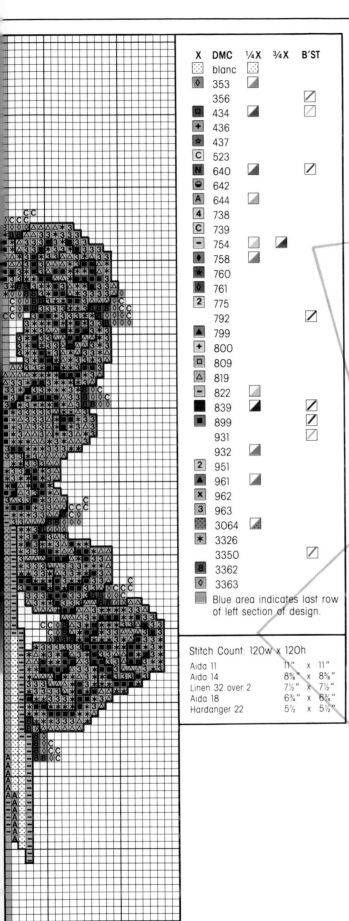

X	DMC	¼X	¾X	B'ST
⠒	blanc	⠒		
◇	353	◩		
	356			◩
▫	434	◩		◩
+	436			
✿	437			
C	523	◩		◩
N	640	◩		◩
◉	642			
A	644	◩		
4	738			
C	739			
−	754	◩	◩	
◆	758	◩		
★	760			
◈	761			
2	775			
	792			◩
▲	799	◩		
+	800			
▫	809			
△	819			
−	822	◩		
■	839	◩		◩
■	899			◩
	931			◩
	932	◩		
2	951			
▲	961	◩		
✕	962			
3	963			
▦	3064	◩		
✳	3326			
	3350			◩
8	3362			
◇	3363			

▦ Blue area indicates last row of left section of design.

Stitch Count: 120w x 120h

Aida 11	11"	x	11"
Aida 14	8⅝"	x	8⅝"
Linen 32 over 2	7½"	x	7½"
Aida 18	6¾"	x	6¾"
Hardanger 22	5½	x	5½"

Treetop Angel (shown on page 30): The design was stitched over 2 fabric threads on a 14" square of Raw Belfast Linen (32 ct). Two strands of floss were used for Cross Stitch and 1 for Backstitch. It was made into a treetop angel.

For treetop angel, cut one 14" square of Raw Belfast Linen for backing. Cut one 5½" x 8" piece of Raw Belfast Linen for pocket.

Fold tracing paper in half and match fold to dashed line of pattern. Trace pattern onto folded tracing paper; leaving paper folded, cut out pattern. Unfold pattern and press to flatten. With right sides facing and matching raw edges, place stitched piece and backing fabric together. Center pattern on wrong side of stitched piece. Use fabric marking pencil to draw around pattern. Cut out fabric pieces ¼" outside drawn line.

For pocket, press all edges of pocket fabric ½" to one side; press edges ½" to same side again. Using a ¼" seam allowance, sew around all edges. Referring to **Fig. 1**, center pocket on one side of backing fabric; leaving bottom edge open, sew pocket to backing fabric along seamline. This will be right side of backing fabric.

With right sides facing and matching raw edges, pin stitched piece and backing fabric together. Sewing along drawn line and leaving an opening for turning, sew pieces together; clip seam allowance at points. Turn shape right side out. Stuff shape with polyester fiberfill and sew final closure by hand.

Fig. 1

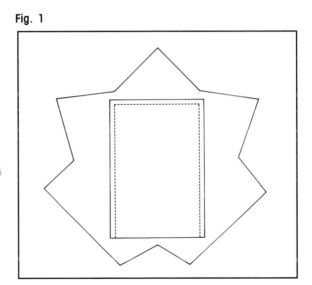

Treetop Angel in Frame (shown on page 31): The design was stitched on a 14" square of Raw Belfast Linen (32 ct). Two strands of floss were used for Cross Stitch and 1 for Backstitch. It was custom framed.

O COME, LET US ADORE HIM

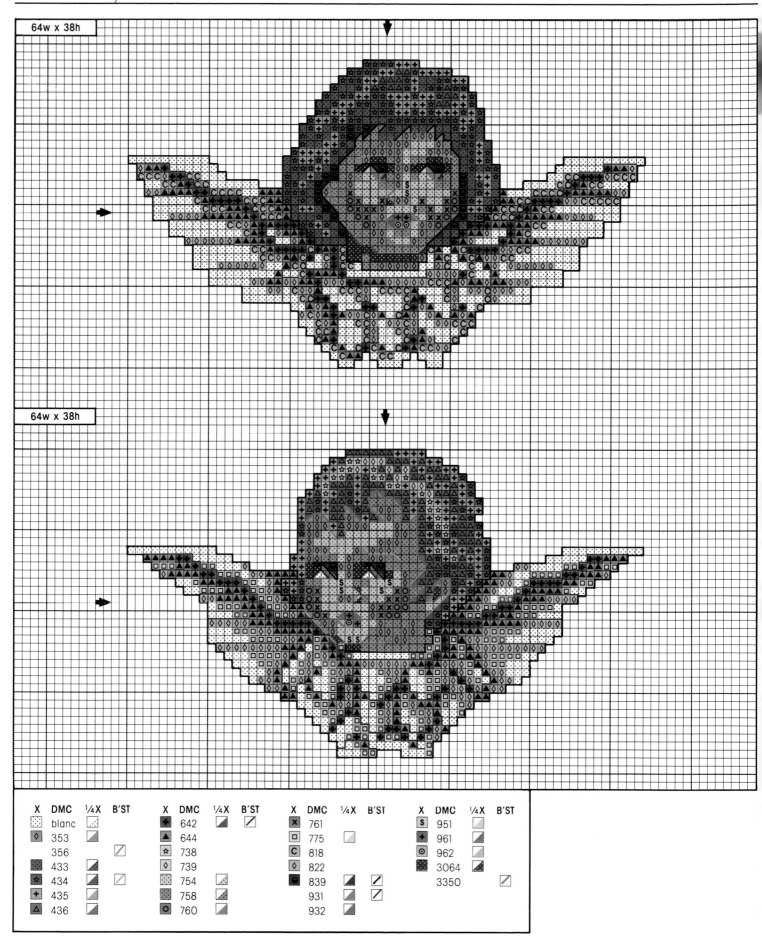

X	DMC	¼X	B'ST		X	DMC	¼X	B'ST		X	DMC	¼X	B'ST		X	DMC	¼X	B'ST		X	DMC	¼X	B'ST
	blanc				✦	642				✕	761				◨	951		
◇	353				▲	644				▣	775				✦	961		
	356				☆	738				C	818				⊙	962		
	433				◇	739				◇	822					3064		
✪	434					754				●	839					3350		
✦	435					758					931							
△	436				⊙	760					932							

64w x 38h

64w x 38h

72

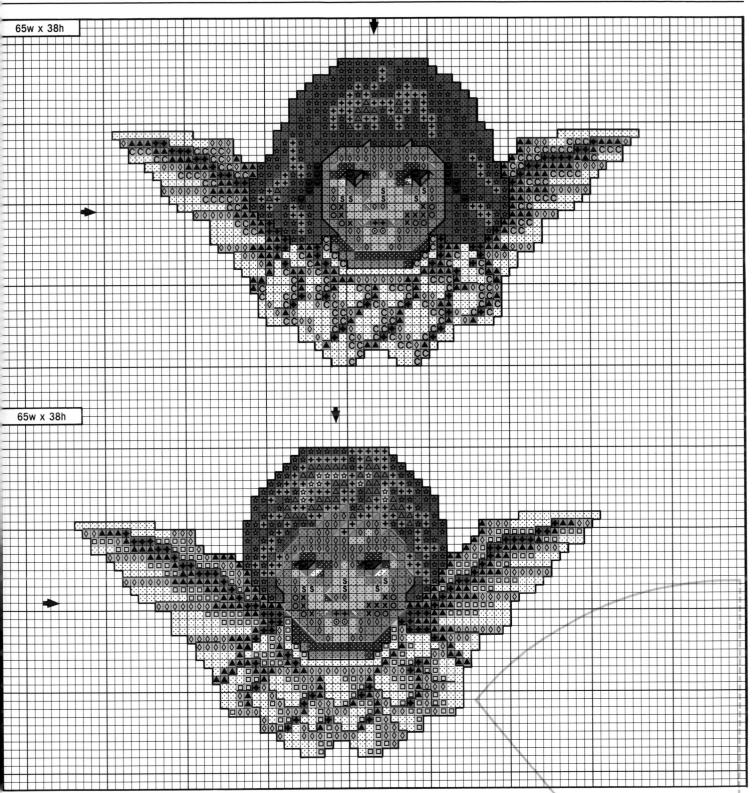

65w x 38h

65w x 38h

Angel Ornaments (shown on page 30): Each design was stitched over 2 fabric threads on a 10" x 7" piece of Raw Belfast Linen (32 ct). Two strands of floss were used for Cross Stitch and 1 for Backstitch. They were made into ornaments.

For each ornament, cut one 10" x 7" piece of Raw Belfast Linen for backing.

Fold tracing paper in half and match fold to dashed line of pattern. Trace pattern onto folded tracing paper; leaving paper folded, cut out pattern. Unfold pattern and press to flatten. With right sides facing and

matching raw edges, place stitched piece and backing fabric together. Center pattern on wrong side of stitched piece. Use fabric marking pencil to draw around pattern.

Leaving an opening for turning and stuffing, sew stitched piece and backing fabric together directly on drawn line. Trim seam allowance to ¼" and clip curves and corners. Turn ornament right side out.

Stuff ornament with polyester fiberfill and sew final closure by hand.

For hanger, cut two 12" lengths of ¹⁄₁₆"w ribbon. Whipstitch one end of each length to one top corner of ornament at seam.

CHRISTMAS IS FOR CHILDREN

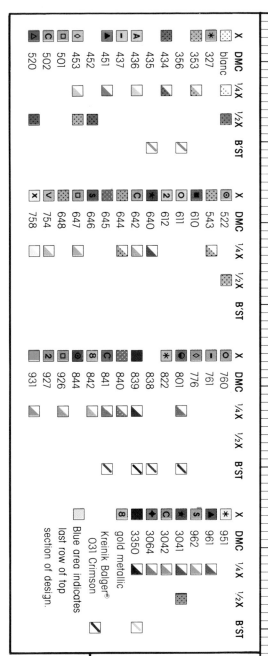

Stitch Count: 99w x 144h

Aida 11	9"	x 13⅛"
Aida 14	7⅛"	x 10⅜"
Linen 32 over 2	6¼"	x 9"
Aida 18	5½"	x 8"
Hardanger 22	4½"	x 6⅝"

Christmas Secrets in Frame (shown on page 35): The design was stitched over 2 fabric threads on a 15" x 18" piece of Cream Belfast Linen (32 ct). Three strands of floss were used for metallic Cross Stitch, 2 for all other Cross Stitch, 1 for Half Cross Stitch, 2 for metallic Backstitch, and 1 for all other Backstitch. It was custom framed.

CHRISTMAS IS FOR CHILDREN

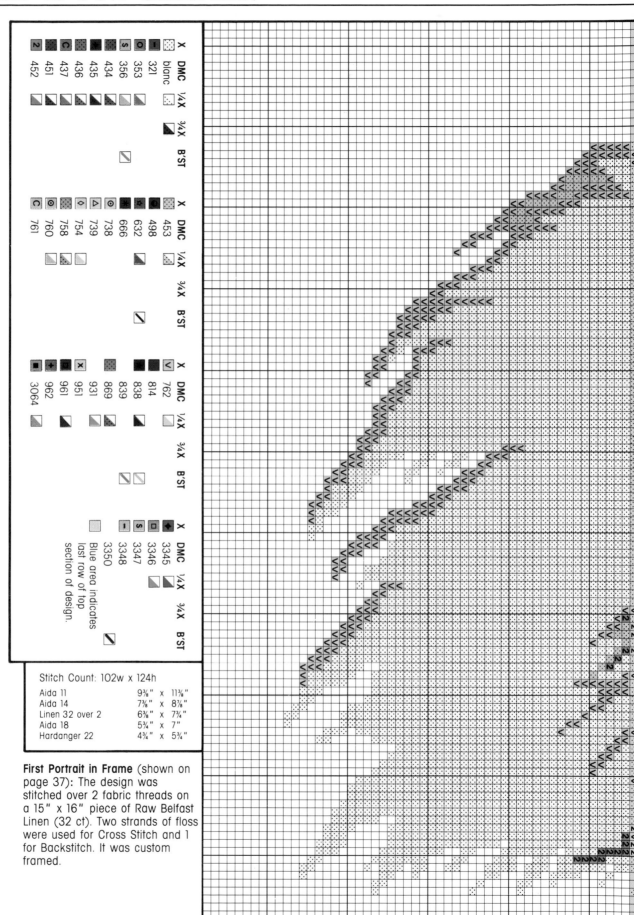

X	DMC	1/4X	3/4X	B'ST
	blanc			
	321			
	353			
	356			
	434			
	435			
	436			
	437			
	451			
	452			

X	DMC	1/4X	3/4X	B'ST
	453			
	498			
	632			
	666			
	738			
	739			
	754			
	758			
	760			
	761			

X	DMC	1/4X	3/4X	B'ST
	762			
	814			
	838			
	839			
	869			
	931			
	951			
	961			
	962			
	3064			

X	DMC	1/4X	3/4X	B'ST
	3350			
	3348			
	3347			
	3346			
	3345			

Blue area indicates last row of top section of design.

Stitch Count: 102w x 124h

Aida 11	9⅜"	x	11⅜"
Aida 14	7⅜"	x	8⅞"
Linen 32 over 2	6⅜"	x	7¾"
Aida 18	5¾"	x	7"
Hardanger 22	4¾"	x	5¾"

First Portrait in Frame (shown on page 37): The design was stitched over 2 fabric threads on a 15" x 16" piece of Raw Belfast Linen (32 ct). Two strands of floss were used for Cross Stitch and 1 for Backstitch. It was custom framed.

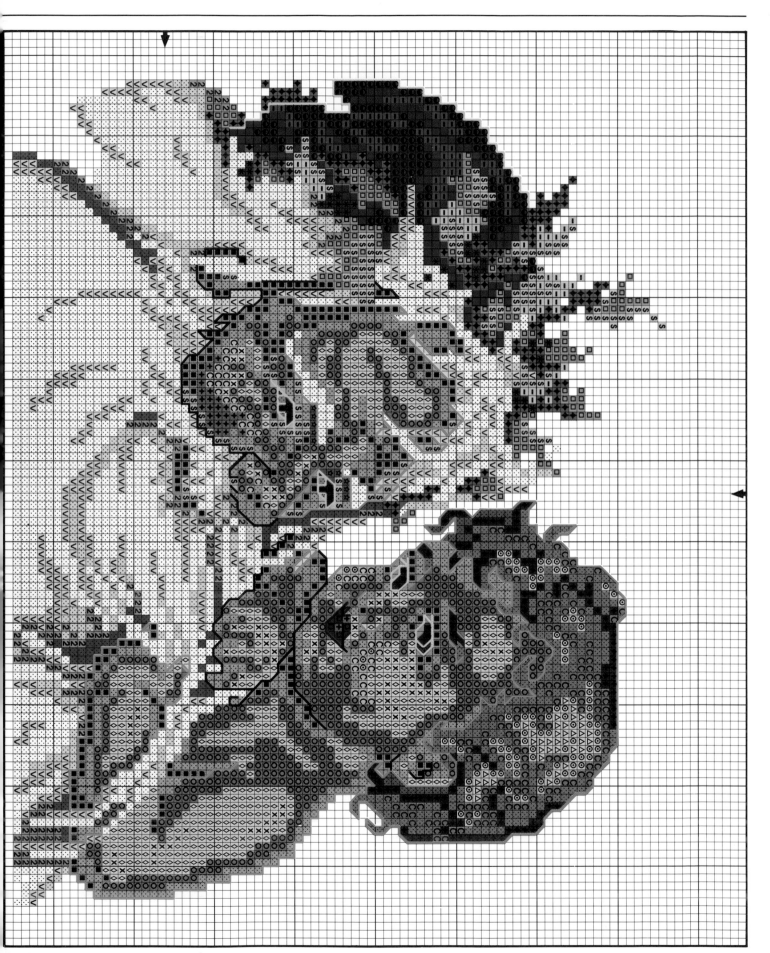

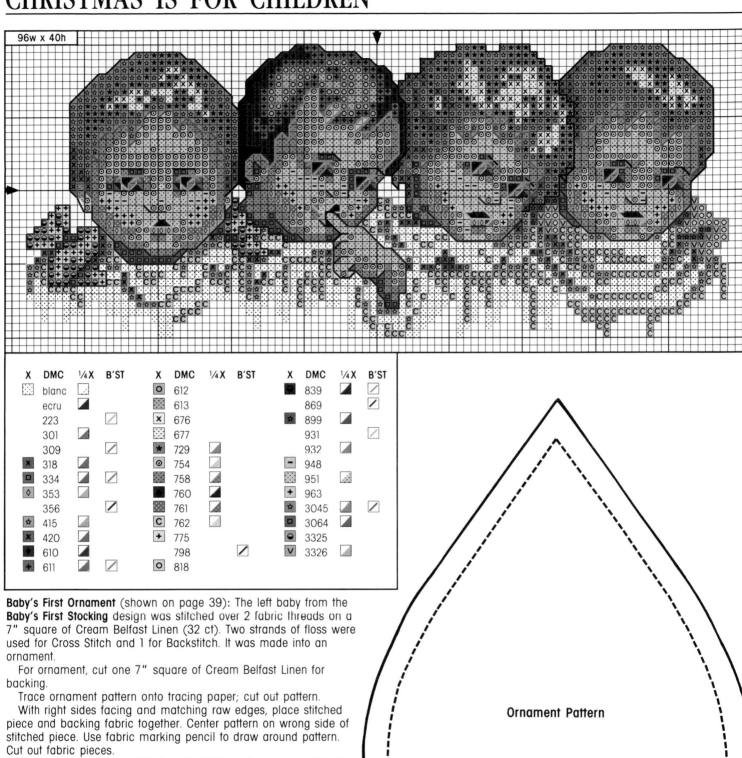

96w x 40h

X	DMC	1/4X	B'ST	X	DMC	1/4X	B'ST	X	DMC	1/4X	B'ST
	blanc			○	612			■	839		
	ecru	◣			613				869		
	223		◹	×	676			★	899	◣	
	301	◣			677				931		
	309		◹	★	729	◣			932	◣	
×	318	◣		◉	754	◣		−	948		
□	334	◣	◹		758	◣			951		
◇	353	◣		■	760	◣		+	963		
	356		◹		761	◣		★	3045	◣	◹
★	415	◣		C	762	◣		□	3064	◣	
×	420	◣		+	775			◎	3325		
■	610	◣			798		◹	V	3326	◣	
+	611	◣	◹	○	818						

Baby's First Ornament (shown on page 39): The left baby from the **Baby's First Stocking** design was stitched over 2 fabric threads on a 7" square of Cream Belfast Linen (32 ct). Two strands of floss were used for Cross Stitch and 1 for Backstitch. It was made into an ornament.

For ornament, cut one 7" square of Cream Belfast Linen for backing.

Trace ornament pattern onto tracing paper; cut out pattern.

With right sides facing and matching raw edges, place stitched piece and backing fabric together. Center pattern on wrong side of stitched piece. Use fabric marking pencil to draw around pattern. Cut out fabric pieces.

For lace ruffle, cut one 14" length of 1"w gathered lace. Matching edges and beginning at top of stitched piece, use a 1/4" seam allowance to sew lace to right side of stitched piece.

For hanger, cut one 9" length of 1/8"w ribbon. Fold ribbon in half. Pin ends to right side of stitched piece, even with top edge of stitched piece.

With right sides facing and matching raw edges, pin stitched piece and backing fabric together. Using a 1/4" seam allowance and leaving an opening for turning, sew pieces together (being careful not to catch ribbon in stitching); clip seam allowance at curves and corners. Turn shape right side out. Stuff shape with polyester fiberfill and sew final closure by hand.

Cut one 10" length of 1/8"w ribbon and tie in a bow. Sew bow to top of ornament.

Ornament Pattern

Baby's First Stocking (shown on page 38): The design was centered and stitched over 1 fabric thread on a 13½" x 5" piece of Ivory Hardanger (22 ct), with left edge of design 1½" from one short edge of fabric. One strand of floss was used for Cross Stitch and for Backstitch. It was made into a stocking.

For stocking, cut one 13½" x 5" piece of Ivory Hardanger for cuff backing. Cut two 11" x 18" pieces of fabric for stocking. Cut two 11" x 18" pieces of fabric for lining.

Matching arrows to form one pattern, trace entire stocking pattern onto tracing paper; cut out pattern. With right sides facing and matching raw edges, place stocking fabric pieces together. Place pattern on wrong side of one fabric piece and use fabric marking pencil to draw around pattern. Cutting through both layers, cut out stocking pieces. Repeat for lining pieces, cutting just inside drawn line.

With right sides facing and matching raw edges, pin stocking pieces together. Using a ½" seam allowance and leaving top edge open, sew pieces together; clip seam allowance at curves.

With right sides facing and matching raw edges, pin lining pieces together. Using a ½" seam allowance and leaving top edge open, sew pieces together; clip seam allowance at curves. **Do not turn lining right side out.** Press top edge of lining ½" to wrong side.

With right sides facing and matching short edges, fold each cuff piece in half. Using a ½" seam allowance, sew along short edges of each piece.

For cording, cut one 2" x 15" bias strip of coordinating fabric.

Lay purchased cord along center of strip on wrong side of fabric; matching raw edges, fold strip over cord. Using zipper foot, baste along length of strip close to cord; trim seam allowance to ½". Matching raw edges and beginning at seam, pin cording to right side at bottom of stitched piece. Ends of cording should overlap approximately 2"; pin overlapping end out of the way.

Starting 2" from beginning end of cording, baste cording to stitched piece.

On overlapping end of cording, remove 2½" of basting; fold end of fabric back and trim cord so that it meets beginning end of cord. Fold end of fabric under ½"; wrap fabric over beginning end of cording. Finish basting cording to stitched piece.

For face ruffle, cut one 14" length of 1¼"w gathered lace. Matching edges and beginning at cuff seam, baste lace to right side of stitched piece along basting line of cording.

With right sides facing and matching raw edges, use a ½" seam allowance to sew cuff pieces together along edge with cording and lace. Turn right side out and press.

With right side of cuff (side with cording) and wrong side of stocking facing, match raw edges and use a ½" seam allowance to sew cuff to stocking. Fold cuff 3" over stocking; press.

For hanger, cut one 7" length of purchased cord. Fold cord in half and whipstitch to inside of stocking at left.

With wrong sides facing and matching edges, place lining inside stocking. Matching pressed edge of lining to seam of cuff, whipstitch lining to stocking.

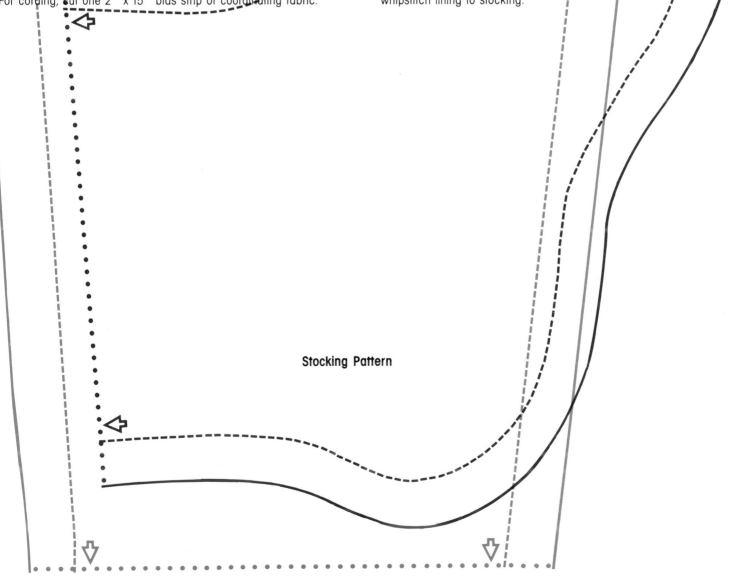

Stocking Pattern

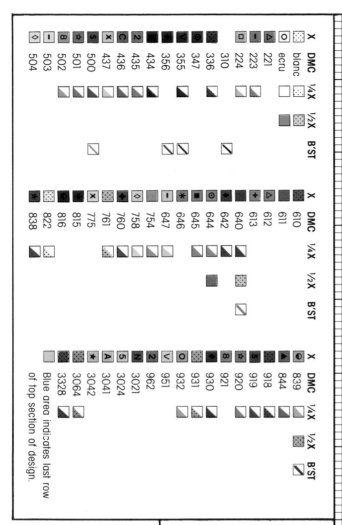

Stitch Count: 108w x 148h

Aida 11	9⅞"	x 13½"
Aida 14	7¾"	x 10⅝"
Linen 32 over 2	6¾"	x 9¼"
Aida 18	6"	x 8¼"
Hardanger 22	5"	x 6¾"

A Glimpse of the Gentleman Stocking (shown on page 40): The design was centered and stitched over 2 fabric threads on a 14" x 21" piece of Cream Belfast Linen (32 ct), with bottom of design 3½" from one short edge of fabric. Two strands of floss were used for Cross Stitch, 1 for Half Cross Stitch, and 1 for Backstitch. It was made into a stocking (see Stocking instructions, page 82).

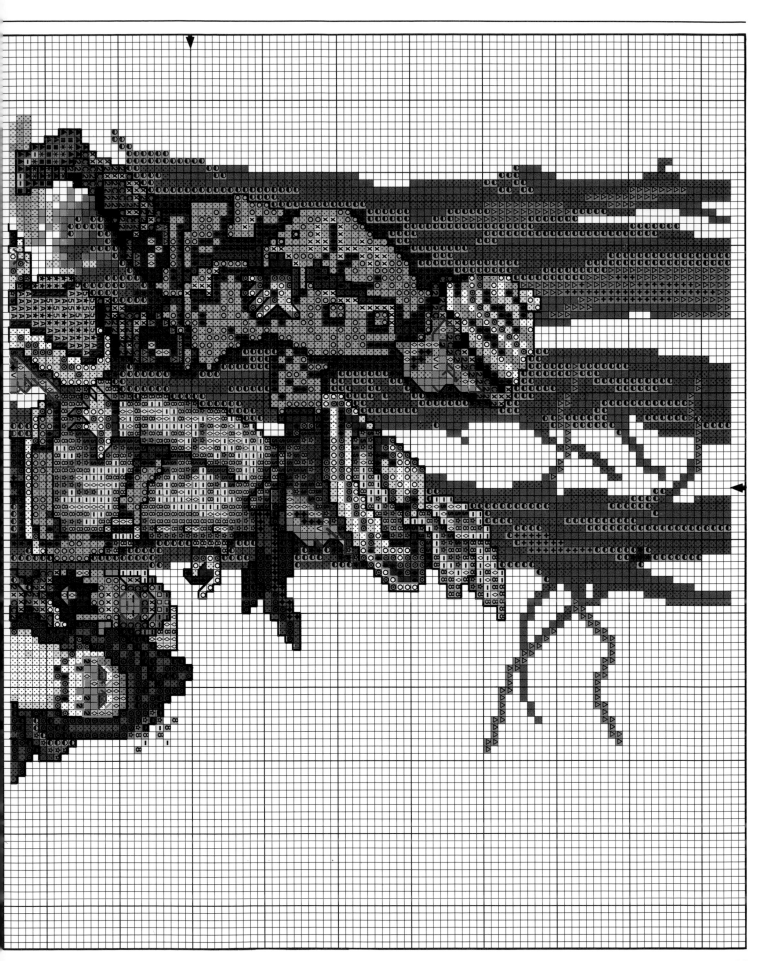

CHRISTMAS IS FOR CHILDREN

A Glimpse of the Gentleman Stocking
Chart on pages 80-81.

For stocking, cut one 14" x 21" piece of Cream Belfast Linen for backing. Cut two 14" x 21" pieces of off-white fabric for lining. Cut two 5½" x 15" pieces of coordinating fabric for cuff.

Matching arrows to form one pattern, trace entire stocking pattern onto tracing paper; cut out pattern. With right sides facing and matching raw edges, place stitched piece and backing fabric together. Place pattern on wrong side of stitched piece. Refer to photo to position pattern on design; pin pattern in place. Use fabric marking pencil to draw around pattern.

Leaving top edge open, sew stitched piece and backing fabric together directly on drawn line. Trim seam allowance to ½" and clip curves. Trim top edge along drawn line. Turn stocking right side out.

Repeat to draw around pattern and sew lining pieces together, sewing just inside drawn line. Trim seam allowance to ½" and clip curves. Trim top edge along drawn line. **Do not turn lining right side out.** Press top edge of lining ½" to wrong side.

With right sides facing and matching short edges, fold each cuff piece in half. Using a ½" seam allowance, sew along short edges of each piece.

For cording, cut one 2" x 18" bias strip of coordinating fabric. Lay purchased cord along center of strip on wrong side of fabric; matching raw edges, fold strip over cord. Using zipper foot, baste along length of strip close to cord; trim seam allowance to ½". Matching raw edges and beginning at cuff seam, pin cording to

right side of one cuff piece. Ends of cording should overlap approximately 2"; pin overlapping end out of the way.

Starting 2" from beginning end of cording, baste cording to cuff piece.

On overlapping end of cording, remove 2½" of basting; fold end of fabric back and trim cord so that it meets beginning end of cord. Fold end of fabric under ½"; wrap fabric over beginning end of cording. Finish basting cording to cuff piece.

For lace ruffle, cut one 15" length of 1⅞"w flat lace. Matching edges and beginning at cuff seam, baste lace to right side of cuff piece along basting line of cording.

With right sides facing and matching raw edges, use a ½" seam allowance to sew cuff pieces together along edge with cording and lace. Turn right side out and press.

With right side of cuff (side with cording) and wrong side of stocking facing, match raw edges and use a ½" seam allowance to sew cuff to stocking. Fold cuff 3½" over stocking; press.

For hanger, cut one 1" x 6" strip of coordinating fabric. Press each long edge of strip ¼" to center. Matching long edges, fold strip in half and sew close to folded edges. Matching short edges, fold hanger in half and whipstitch to inside of stocking at left seam.

With wrong sides facing and matching edges, place lining inside stocking. Matching pressed edge of lining to seam of cuff, whipstitch lining to stocking.

Stocking Pattern

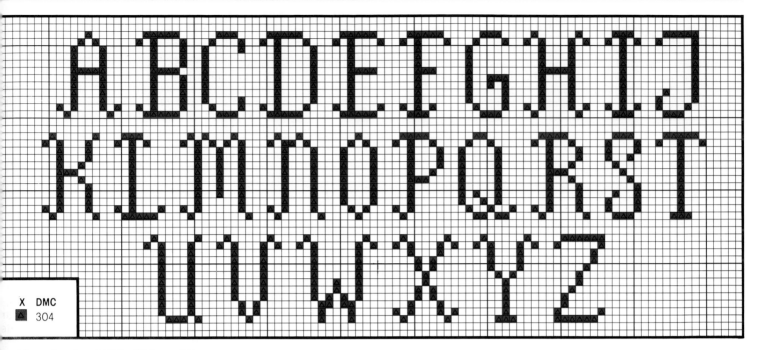

X	DMC
▲	304

Stockings for Good Little Girls and Boys
Chart on page 84; pattern on page 82.

For stocking, cut one 15½" x 6¾" piece of Cream Belfast Linen for cuff backing. Cut two 14" x 21" pieces of fabric for stocking. Cut two 14" x 21" pieces of fabric for lining.

Matching arrows to form one pattern, trace entire stocking pattern onto tracing paper; cut out pattern. With right sides facing and matching raw edges, place stocking fabric pieces together. Place pattern on wrong side of one fabric piece and use fabric marking pencil to draw around pattern.

Leaving top edge open, sew stocking pieces together directly on drawn line. Trim seam allowance to ½" and clip curves. Trim top edge along drawn line. Turn stocking right side out.

Repeat to draw around pattern and sew lining pieces together, sewing just inside drawn line. Trim seam allowance to ½" and clip curves. Trim top edge along drawn line. **Do not turn lining right side out.** Press top edge of lining ½" to wrong side.

With right sides facing and matching short edges, fold each cuff piece in half. Using a ½" seam allowance, sew along short edges of each piece.

For cording, cut one 2" x 18" bias strip of coordinating fabric. Lay purchased cord along center of strip on wrong side of fabric; matching raw edges, fold strip over cord. Using zipper foot, baste along length of strip close to cord; trim seam allowance to ½". Matching raw edges and beginning at seam, pin cording to right side at bottom of stitched piece. Ends of cording should overlap approximately 2"; pin overlapping end out of the way.

Starting 2" from beginning end of cording, baste cording to stitched piece.

On overlapping end of cording, remove 2½" of basting; fold end of fabric back and trim cord so that it meets beginning end of cord. Fold end of fabric under ½"; wrap fabric over beginning end of cording. Finish basting cording to stitched piece.

For lace ruffle on girl stocking, cut one 15" length of ¾"w flat lace. Matching edges and beginning at cuff seam, baste lace to right side of stitched piece along basting line of cording.

With right sides facing and matching raw edges, use a ½" seam allowance to sew cuff pieces together along edge with cording and lace. Turn right side out and press.

With right side of cuff (side with cording) and wrong side of stocking facing, match raw edges and use a ½" seam allowance to sew cuff to stocking. Fold cuff 3½" over stocking; press.

For hanger, cut one 1" x 6" strip of coordinating fabric. Press each long edge of strip ¼" to center. Matching long edges, fold strip in half and sew close to folded edges. Matching short edges, fold hanger in half and whipstitch to inside of stocking at left seam.

With wrong sides facing and matching edges, place lining inside stocking. Matching pressed edge of lining to seam of cuff, whipstitch lining to stocking.

THE MERRIE CHRISTMAS DAYS

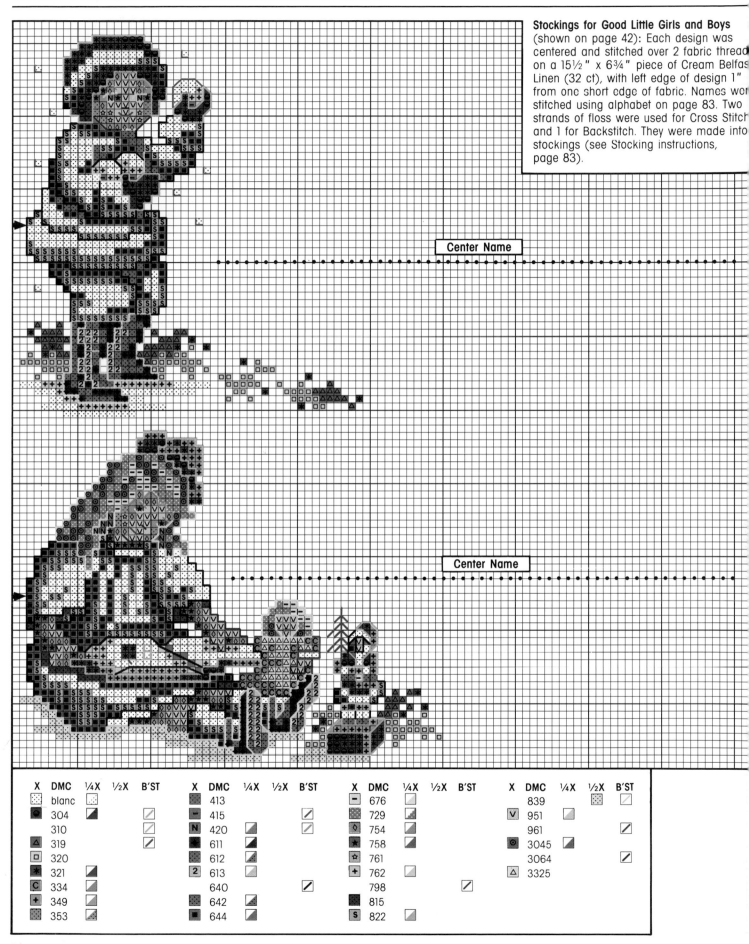

Stockings for Good Little Girls and Boys (shown on page 42): Each design was centered and stitched over 2 fabric thread on a 15½" x 6¾" piece of Cream Belfas Linen (32 ct), with left edge of design 1" from one short edge of fabric. Names wer stitched using alphabet on page 83. Two strands of floss were used for Cross Stitch and 1 for Backstitch. They were made into stockings (see Stocking instructions, page 83).

Center Name

Center Name

X	DMC	¼X	½X	B'ST	X	DMC	¼X	½X	B'ST	X	DMC	¼X	½X	B'ST	X	DMC	¼X	½X	B'ST
	blanc					413				-	676					839			
	304					415					729				V	951			
	310				N	420				◊	754					961			
△	319					611				★	758				◉	3045			
□	320					612				☆	761					3064			
✳	321				2	613				+	762				△	3325			
C	334					640					798								
+	349					642					815								
	353					644				S	822								

84

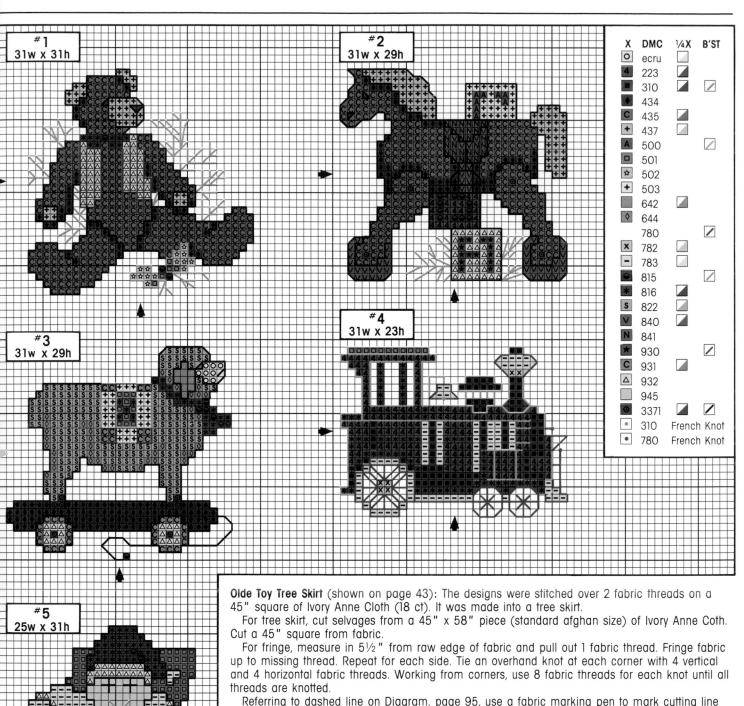

X	DMC	1/4X	B'ST
○	ecru		
4	223		
■	310	◪	◿
◆	434		
C	435	◪	
+	437	◪	
A	500		◿
□	501		
☆	502		
+	503		
▨	642	◪	
◇	644		
	780		◿
X	782	◪	
−	783	◪	
◉	815		◿
✱	816	◪	
S	822	◪	
V	840	◪	
N	841		
★	930		◿
C	931	◪	
△	932		
▨	945		
◉	3371	◪	◿
⊡	310		French Knot
⊡	780		French Knot

Olde Toy Tree Skirt (shown on page 43): The designs were stitched over 2 fabric threads on a 45" square of Ivory Anne Cloth (18 ct). It was made into a tree skirt.

For tree skirt, cut selvages from a 45" x 58" piece (standard afghan size) of Ivory Anne Coth. Cut a 45" square from fabric.

For fringe, measure in 5½" from raw edge of fabric and pull out 1 fabric thread. Fringe fabric up to missing thread. Repeat for each side. Tie an overhand knot at each corner with 4 vertical and 4 horizontal fabric threads. Working from corners, use 8 fabric threads for each knot until all threads are knotted.

Referring to dashed line on Diagram, page 95, use a fabric marking pen to mark cutting line on fabric. Referring to grey line on Diagram, sew ½" from cutting line. Following cutting line, cut opening in tree skirt. Clip corners of center opening up to stitching line. Press raw edges ¼" to wrong side; press under ¼" again and hem. Apply stitchless fabric glue to wrong side at corners of center opening and allow to dry.

Refer to Diagram for placement of designs on fabric; use 6 strands of floss for Cross Stitch, 2 for Backstitch, and 2 for French Knots.

Olde Toy Ornaments (shown on page 43): Each design was stitched over 2 fabric threads on a 7" square of Cream Lugana (25 ct). Three strands of floss were used for Cross Stitch, 1 for Backstitch, and 1 for French Knots. They were made into fringed mini pillow ornaments.

For each ornament, cut stitched piece 1" larger than design on all sides. Cut one piece of Cream Lugana same size as stitched piece for backing.

With wrong sides facing, use desired floss color to cross stitch fabric pieces together ½" from sides and bottom edge. Stuff with polyester fiberfill.

For hanger, fold a 5½" length of 1/16"w ribbon in half; place ribbon ends between fabric pieces in center of top edge. Catching ribbon ends in stitching, cross stitch across top of mini pillow ½" from edge. Fringe fabric to cross-stitched lines.

82w x 96h

X	DMC	¼X	B'ST		X	DMC	¼X	B'ST		X	DMC	¼X	B'ST
-	225				O	727				N	977		
C	320				☆	760				◉	3328		
✴	347				-	761				☐	gold		
★	367				◕	814		✓			metallic		
+	368				✳	815				●	370		French Knot
	370		✓		S	895		✓					

Christmas Album (shown on page 44): The design was stitched over 2 fabric threads on a 9" x 10" piece of Cream Belfast Linen (32 ct). Two strands of floss were used for Cross Stitch, 4 for metallic Cross Stitch, and 1 for Backstitch. It was applied to the front of a fabric covered photo album.

For Christmas album, cut stitched piece 1¾" larger than design on all sides. Cut one 40½" x 12½" piece of fabric to cover an 11"w x 11½"h album with a 1½" spine. Cut one 39½" x 11½" piece of fusible web and one 39½" x 11½" piece of craft batting.

Center web, then batting on wrong side of fabric; follow manufacturer's instructions to fuse batting to fabric. Press short edges of fabric ½" to wrong side (over edges of batting) and glue to batting.

To form pockets for album, press one short edge of fabric approx. 9" to right side; press remaining short edge 7" to right size (adjust pocket sizes as necessary to fit individual albums). Using a ½" seam allowance, sew across top and bottom of pockets; clip corners. Turn cover right side out. Fold remaining raw edges to wrong side and glue to batting; allow glue to dry. Slip front cover of album into large pocket and back cover into small pocket.

To pad stitched piece, cut a piece of cardboard ¾" larger than design on all sides. Cut a piece of craft batting same size as cardboard. Place batting on cardboard; center stitched piece on batting. Fold edges of stitched piece to back of cardboard and glue in place; allow glue to dry.

For cording around stitched piece, cut one 2" x 34" bias strip of gold lamé fabric. Lay purchased cord along center of strip on wrong side of fabric; matching raw edges, fold strip over cord. Using zipper foot, baste along length of strip close to cord; trim seam allowance to ½". Starting 2" from beginning of cording and at bottom center of stitched piece, glue cording to back of stitched piece; stop 3" from overlapping end of cording.

On overlapping end of cording, remove 2½" of basting; fold end of fabric back and trim cord so that it meets beginning end of cord. Fold end of fabric under ½"; wrap fabric over beginning end of cording. Finish gluing cording to stitched piece.

Center and glue padded stitched piece to front of covered album; allow glue to dry.

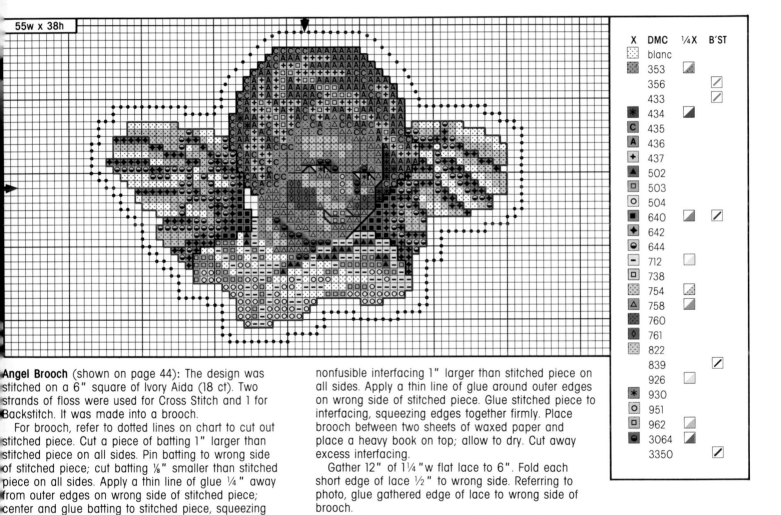

55w x 38h

X	DMC	¼X	B'ST
	blanc		
	353	◩	
	356		◪
	433		◪
✳	434	◩	
C	435		
A	436		
✚	437		
▲	502		
◻	503		
◎	504		
■	640	◨	◪
◆	642		
⊖	644		
−	712	◱	
◻	738		
	754	◩	
△	758	◩	
▨	760		
◈	761		
	822		
	839		◪
	926	◱	
✳	930		
◎	951		
▣	962		◩
◕	3064	◨	
	3350		◪

Angel Brooch (shown on page 44): The design was stitched on a 6" square of Ivory Aida (18 ct). Two strands of floss were used for Cross Stitch and 1 for Backstitch. It was made into a brooch.

For brooch, refer to dotted lines on chart to cut out stitched piece. Cut a piece of batting 1" larger than stitched piece on all sides. Pin batting to wrong side of stitched piece; cut batting ⅛" smaller than stitched piece on all sides. Apply a thin line of glue ¼" away from outer edges on wrong side of stitched piece; center and glue batting to stitched piece, squeezing edges together firmly. Cut a piece of heavy weight, nonfusible interfacing 1" larger than stitched piece on all sides. Apply a thin line of glue around outer edges on wrong side of stitched piece. Glue stitched piece to interfacing, squeezing edges together firmly. Place brooch between two sheets of waxed paper and place a heavy book on top; allow to dry. Cut away excess interfacing.

Gather 12" of 1¼"w flat lace to 6". Fold each short edge of lace ½" to wrong side. Referring to photo, glue gathered edge of lace to wrong side of brooch.

Glue 1" pin back to wrong side of brooch.

THE MERRIE CHRISTMAS DAYS

64w x 31h

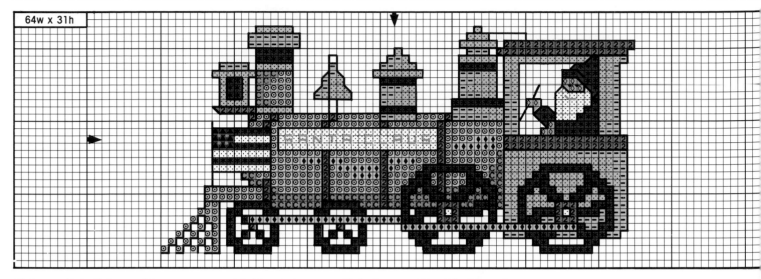

Christmas Train Pajamas (shown on page 47): The design was stitched over a 7" x 5" piece of waste canvas (16 ct) on a boy's sweatshirt. Three strands of floss were used for Cross Stitch, 1 for Backstitch, and 1 for French Knots. (See Working on Waste Canvas, page 95.)

57w x 38h   19w x 24h

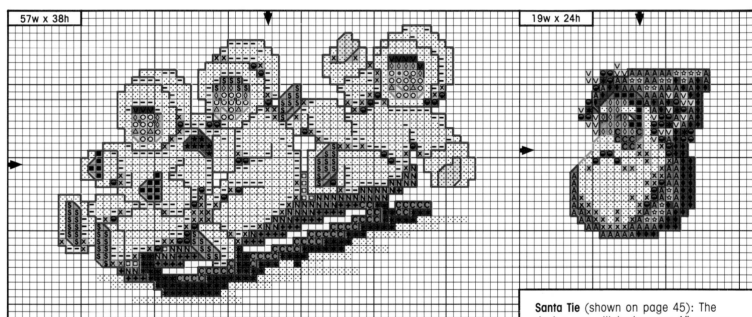

Snowbunny Gown (shown on page 47): The design was stitched over an 8" x 6" piece of waste canvas (16 ct) on a girl's gown (made from McCall's Pattern #3450). Three strands of floss were used for Cross Stitch, 1 for Backstitch, and 1 for French Knots. (See Working on Waste Canvas, page 95.)

Santa Tie (shown on page 45): The design was stitched over a 4" square of waste canvas (16 ct) on a purchased tie. Three strands of floss were used for Cross Stitch and 1 for Backstitch. (See Working on Waste Canvas, page 95.)

X	DMC	¼X	B'ST	X	DMC	¼X	B'ST	X	DMC	¼X	B'ST	X	DMC	¼X	B'ST
	blanc			✦	420			2	782			◊	930		
−	ecru			☆	422			−	783			○	948		
	310				640			□	797			C	962		
✱	317			◕	644			N	798			■	986		
C	318			S	680			+	799				988		
◔	319				725			X	822			A	3045		
V	320			◊	754			★	824				3350		
✱	321			■	758				839			•	blanc	French Knot
▲	336			△	761				844			•	310	French Knot
◉	415			◆	762			V	869			•	844	French Knot

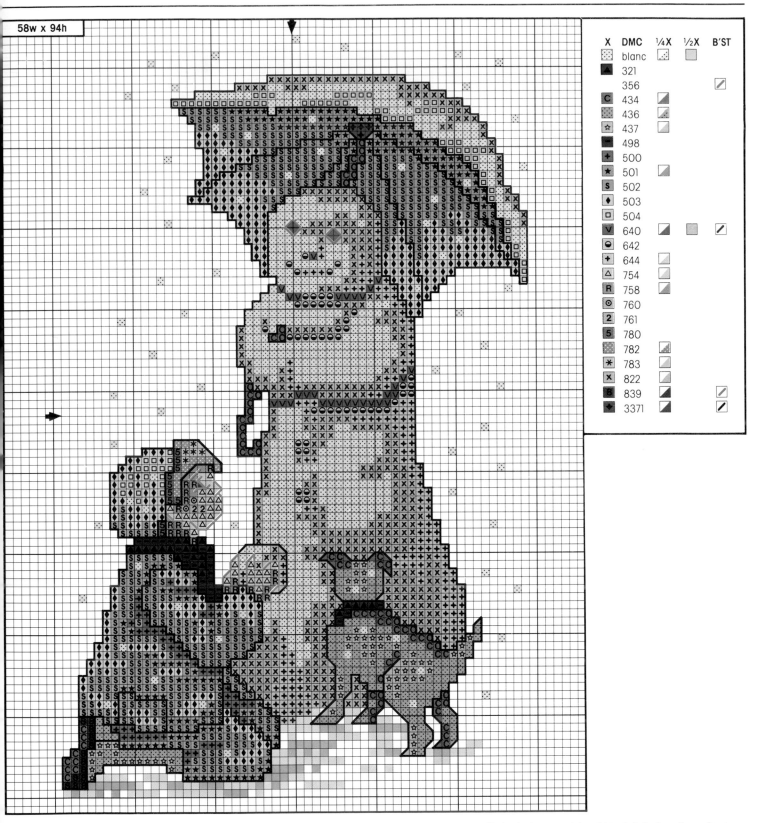

58w x 94h

X	DMC	¼X	½X	B'ST
	blanc			
▲	321			
	356			/
C	434	◢		
	436	◢		
☆	437	◢		
	498			
+	500			
★	501	◢		
S	502			
◆	503			
□	504			
V	640	◢	■	/
●	642			
+	644	◢		
△	754	◢		
R	758	◢		
⊙	760			
2	761			
5	780			
	782	◢		
*	783	◢		
X	822	◢		
8	839	◢		/
✦	3371	◢		/

Christmas Bag (shown on page 45): The design was centered and stitched on a 7" x 15" piece of Raw Belfast Linen (32 ct), with bottom of design 3" from one short edge of fabric. Two strands of floss were used for Cross Stitch, 1 for Half Cross Stitch, and 1 for Backstitch. It was made into a bag.

For bag, cut one 7" x 15" piece of Raw Belfast Linen for backing. With right sides facing and matching raw edges, pin stitched piece and backing fabric together. Using a ½" seam

allowance, sew stitched piece and backing fabric together along sides and bottom. Cut corners diagonally. Press top edge of bag 2" to wrong side; whipstitch top edge in place.

Turn bag right side out. Stuff lower two-thirds of bag with polyester fiberfill. Insert floral arrangement in bag.

To gather top of bag, cut three 44" lengths of ⅛"w ribbon. Tie lengths together in a bow around top of bag.

THE MERRIE CHRISTMAS DAYS

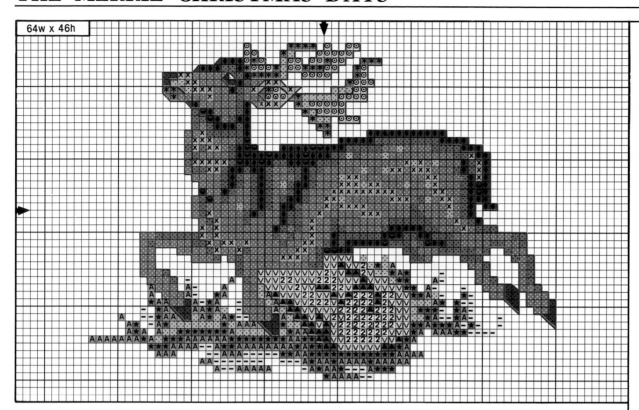

64w x 46h

Winter Warmer for Him (shown on page 46): The design was stitched over a 9" x 7" piece of waste canvas (14 ct) on a purchased scarf. Three strands of floss were used for Cross Stitch and 1 for Backstitch. (See Working on Waste Canvas, page 95.)

80w x 49h

Winter Warmer for Her (shown on page 46): The design was stitched over a 10" x 8" piece of waste canvas (14 ct) on a purchased scarf. Three strands of floss were used for Cross Stitch, 1 for Backstitch, and 1 for French Knots. (See Working on Waste Canvas, page 95.)

X	DMC	1/4X	B'ST
	blanc		
8	223		
⊙	224		
■	310		◪
	319		
A	320		
✳	321		
	356		◪
★	367		
−	368		
	413		◪
	433		
	434		
X	435		
	437		
	498		
▲	611		
V	612		
2	613		
△	647		
	676		
◇	725		
5	729		
✳	738		
⊙	739		
−	754		
O	762		
N	783		◪
C	793		
+	794		
◆	801		
V	814		
●	838		
☆	962		
	3371		◪
•	blanc	French Knot	
•	310	French Knot	
⊙	783	French Knot	

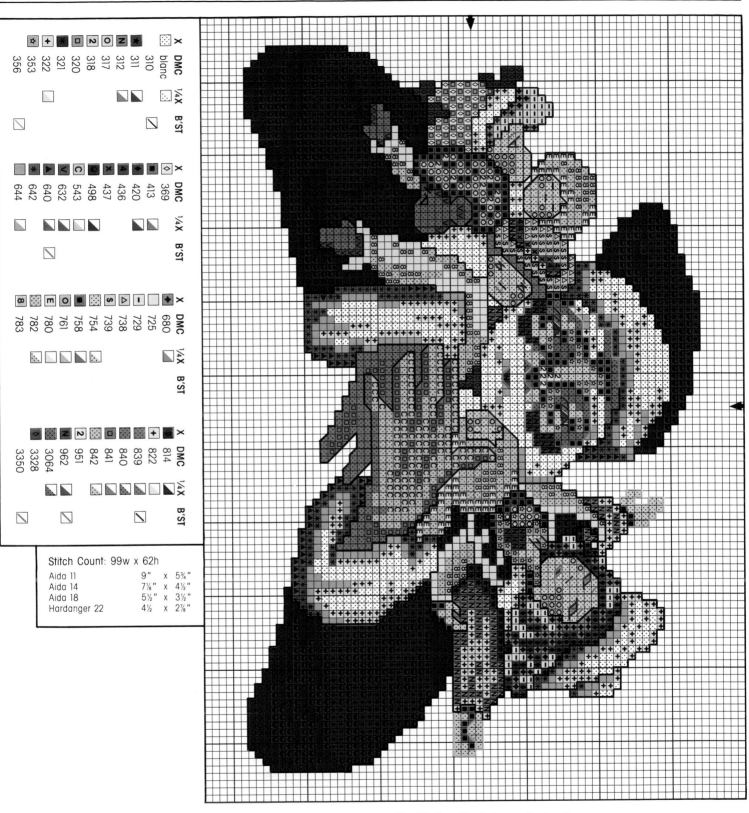

Stitch Count: 99w x 62h

Aida 11	9" x 5¾"
Aida 14	7⅛" x 4½"
Aida 18	5½" x 3½"
Hardanger 22	4½" x 2⅞"

Holiday Basket (shown on page 46): The design was stitched on a 12" x 9" piece of Ivory Aida (14 ct). Two strands of floss were used for Cross Stitch and 1 for Backstitch. It was made into a basket ornament.

For ornament, cut one 12" x 9" piece of Ivory Aida for backing. With right sides facing and leaving an opening at bottom edge for turning and stuffing, sew stitched piece and backing fabric together ¼" from edge of design. Leaving a ¼" seam allowance, cut out ornament; clip curves and turn right side out. Stuff with polyester fiberfill. Sew final closure by hand.

To attach ornament to basket, cut three 10" lengths of ⅛"w ribbon. Refer to photo and use a needle to thread ribbon lengths through bottom of ornament at center and approx. ⅜" from each end. Tie ribbons around basket handle; knot and trim ribbon ends. If desired, decorate basket handle with ribbon and bows.

THE MERRIE CHRISTMAS DAYS

73w x 120h

X	DMC	¼X	½X	B'ST
	blanc			
	310			
S	319			
✳	321			
▲	349			
	351			
N	420			
△	422			
	452			
	498			
X	640			
-	642			
C	644			
O	725			
X	754			
△	758			
C	780			
⊙	781			
	783			
	798			
⊙	799			
+	809			
	814			
S	822			
	839			
☆	962			
◆	3064			
★	3345			
C	3346			
△	3347			
-	3348			

Father Christmas Figure (shown on page 46): The design was stitched on a 12" x 15" piece of Ivory Aida (14 ct). Two strands of floss were used for Cross Stitch, 1 for Half Cross Stitch, and 1 for Backstitch. It was made into a stuffed shape.

For stuffed shape, cut stitched piece 1" larger than design on all sides. Cut a piece of Ivory Aida same size as stitched piece for backing.

With right sides facing and matching raw edges, sew stitched piece and backing fabric together ¼" from design as shown in **Fig. 1**. Leaving a ¼" seam allowance, cut out shape. Clip seam allowance at curves. Turn shape right side out, carefully pushing curves outward.

Baste ½" from raw edge of opening. Stuff shape with polyester fiberfill up to 2" from opening.

To weight bottom, fill a plastic sandwich bag with ½ cup aquarium gravel. Place bag into bottom opening of shape.

For base, cut a 6" square of Ivory Aida. Trace base pattern onto tracing paper; cut out pattern. Center pattern on fabric. Use fabric marking pencil to draw around pattern. Cut out base piece. Baste around piece ½" from raw edge; press raw edge to wrong side along basting line.

Pull basting thread around opening in shape, drawing up gathers so that opening is slightly smaller than base piece. Pin wrong side of base piece over opening in shape. Whipstitch in place, adding fiberfill as necessary to fill bottom of shape.

Fig. 1

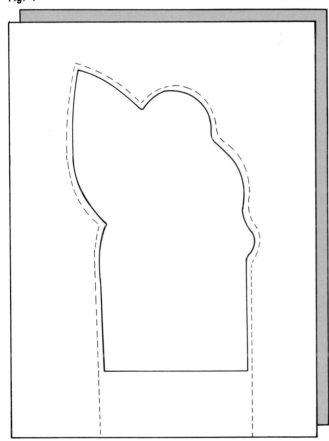

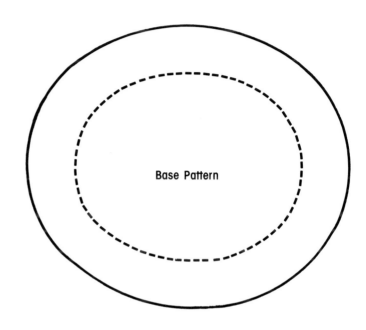

Base Pattern

GENERAL INSTRUCTIONS

WORKING WITH CHARTS

How to Read Charts: Each of the designs is shown in chart form. Each colored square on the chart represents one Cross Stitch. In most cases, the colored square also contains a symbol. However, when a Backstitch line crosses the square, the symbol is omitted. The straight lines on the chart indicate Backstitch. These lines are shown either in color or black; the color of floss to use is indicated in the color key.

STITCH DIAGRAMS

Counted Cross Stitch (X): Work one Cross Stitch to correspond to each colored square on the chart. For horizontal rows, work stitches in two journeys (**Fig. 1**). For vertical rows, complete each stitch as shown (**Fig. 2**). When working over 2 fabric threads, work Cross Stitch as shown in **Fig. 3**. When the chart shows a Backstitch crossing a colored square (**Fig. 4**), a Cross Stitch should be worked first; then the Backstitch should be worked on top of the Cross Stitch.

Fig. 1   **Fig. 2**

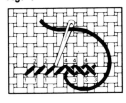

Fig. 3   **Fig. 4**

Quarter Stitch (¼X and ¾X): Quarter Stitches are denoted by triangular shapes of color on the chart and on the color key. Come up at 1 (**Fig. 5**); then split fabric thread to go down at 2. When stitches 1-4 are worked in the same color, the resulting stitch is called a Three-Quarter Stitch (¾X). **Fig. 6** shows the technique for Quarter Stitches when working over 2 fabric threads.

Fig. 5   **Fig. 6**

Half Cross Stitch (½X): This stitch is one journey of the Cross Stitch and is worked from lower left to upper right. **Fig. 7** shows the Half Cross Stitch worked over 2 fabric threads.

Fig. 7

Backstitch (B'ST): For outline detail, Backstitch (shown on chart and on color key by black or colored straight lines) should be worked after the design has been completed (**Fig. 8**).

Fig. 8

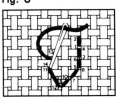

French Knot: Bring needle up at 1. Wrap floss once around needle and insert needle at 2, holding end of floss with non-stitching fingers (**Fig. 9**). Tighten knot; then pull needle through fabric holding floss until it must be released. For larger knot, use more strands; wrap only once.

Fig. 9

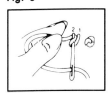

Four-Sided Stitch: Beginning at right edge of fabric, follow **Fig. 10** to come up at 1 and firmly pull fabric threads toward 2. Go down at 2 and firmly pull toward 1. Come up at 3 and firmly pull toward 4. Go down at 4 and firmly pull toward 3. Continue to form a square. (**Note:** Always work vertical stitches from top to bottom and horizontal stitches from left to right to keep tension on fabric threads.)

Fig. 10

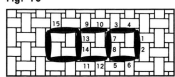

Herringbone Stitch: Begin by coming up at 1 (**Fig. 11**). Then go down at even numbers and come up at odd numbers.

Fig. 11

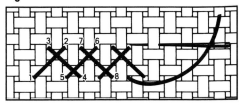

Algerian Eye Stitch: Beginning at right edge of fabric, use a needle to open up a tiny hole at center point ("eye"). Follow **Fig. 12** to come up at 1; firmly pull on "eye" and go down at 2. Come up at 1 again; firmly pull on "eye" and go down at 4. Continue to complete stitch.

Fig. 12

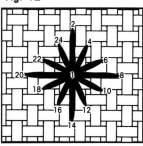

STITCHING TIPS

Working Over Two Fabric Threads: Using a hoop is optional when working over two fabric threads. To work without a hoop, roll the excess fabric from left to right until working area is in the proper position. Using the sewing method instead of the stab method, work stitches over two fabric threads on the front of the fabric. To add support to the stitches, it is important that the first Cross Stitch is placed on the fabric with stitch 1-2 beginning and ending where a vertical fabric thread crosses over a horizontal fabric thread (**Fig. 13**). When the first stitch is in the correct position, the entire design will be placed properly, with vertical fabric threads supporting each stitch.

Fig. 13

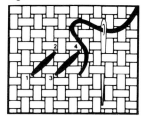

Working on Perforated Paper: Perforated paper has a right and wrong side. The right side is smoother and stitching should be done on this side. Do not fold paper. To find the center, use a ruler to measure width and height, then mark paper lightly with a pencil at center of these measurements. Find square where lines would intersect and mark center lightly. After stitching, carefully erase visible pencil marks. Perforated paper will tear if handled roughly, therefore, hold paper flat while stitching and do not use a hoop. Begin and end stitching by running floss under several stitches on back; never tie knots. Use the stab method when stitching and keep stitching tension consistent. Thread pulled too tightly may tear the paper. Carry floss across back as little as possible.

Working on Waste Canvas: Waste canvas is a special canvas that provides an evenweave grid for placing stitches on fabric. After the design is worked over the canvas, the canvas threads are removed, leaving the design on the fabric. The canvas is available in several mesh sizes.
1. Cut waste canvas 2" larger than design size on all sides; cover edges of canvas with masking tape. Cut a piece of lightweight, non-fusible interfacing the same size as canvas to provide a firm stitching base.
2. Find desired stitching area on clothing item and mark center of area with a pin. Match center of canvas to pin on clothing item. With canvas threads straight, pin canvas to item; pin interfacing to wrong side. Baste all three thicknesses together.

3. Using a sharp needle, work design, stitching from large holes to large holes.
4. Trim canvas to within ¾" of design. Dampen canvas until it becomes limp. Pull out canvas threads one at a time using tweezers.
5. Trim interfacing close to design.

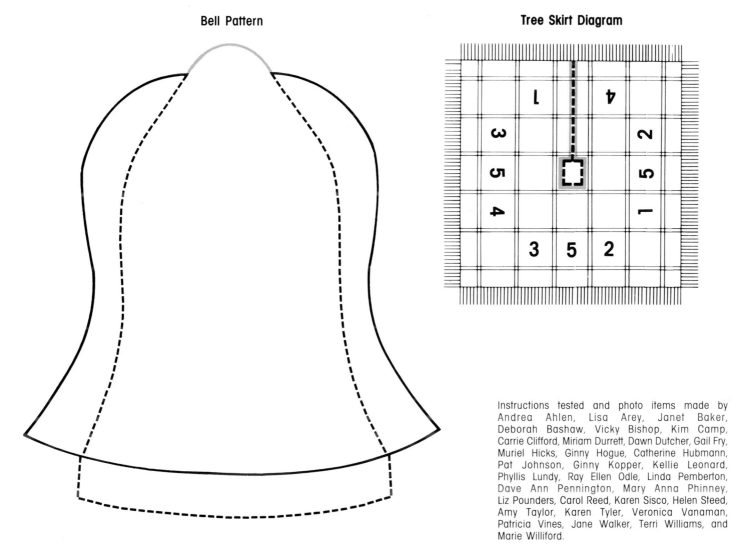

Bell Pattern

Tree Skirt Diagram

Instructions tested and photo items made by Andrea Ahlen, Lisa Arey, Janet Baker, Deborah Bashaw, Vicky Bishop, Kim Camp, Carrie Clifford, Miriam Durrett, Dawn Dutcher, Gail Fry, Muriel Hicks, Ginny Hogue, Catherine Hubmann, Pat Johnson, Ginny Kopper, Kellie Leonard, Phyllis Lundy, Ray Ellen Odle, Linda Pemberton, Dave Ann Pennington, Mary Anna Phinney, Liz Pounders, Carol Reed, Karen Sisco, Helen Steed, Amy Taylor, Karen Tyler, Veronica Vanaman, Patricia Vines, Jane Walker, Terri Williams, and Marie Williford.

MAKE YOUR CHRISTMAS A CELEBRATION OF HEART AND HOME!

- Decorations
- Gifts • Foods

There's something special about handcrafting beautiful decorations for your home, making one-of-a-kind gifts, and creating scrumptious foods for the holidays. Inside the 1990 edition of our 160-page annual book, *The Spirit of Christmas*, you'll find exquisite, full-color photographs and clear, easy-to-follow instructions for each project. What a wonderful Christmas you'll make this year!

Enjoy the new 1990 edition from Leisure Arts
FREE FOR 21 DAYS!

Also Available at Your Local Needlecraft Shop!